Primary School Assemblies

Stories and Ideas

Frank L. Pinfold

Ward Lock Educational

ISBN 0 7062 3881 8

First published 1979

Set in 12 on 13 point Monophoto Bembo
by MS Filmsetting Ltd, Frome, Somerset
and printed by Biddles, Martyr Road, Guildford, Surrey
for Ward Lock Educational
116 Baker Street, London W1M 2BB
A member of the Pentos Group
Made in Great Britain

Contents

Acknowledgments xii

Introduction xiii

1 HELPING OTHERS

1.1 Old George and Lassie 1
A schoolgirl in Grimsby starts a fund to buy a caravan for Old George and his dog.

1.2 Last But Not Least 3
No. 048, the slowest ship in the convoy, but the only one to stop and rescue men whose ships were sunk by U boats.

1.3 New Life in the Camp of Death 5
Self-sacrifice of Angus McGillivray, a POW working on the River Kwai bridge, and the transformation of the prison camp following his example.

1.4 Woodbine Willy 7
Incidents from the life of Geoffrey Studdert Kennedy, chaplain in World War I.

1.5 The X-ray Box 11
How a Tibetan child raised money for the sick Tibetan children in exile in India.

2 PEOPLE OF CHARACTER

2.1 Overcoming a Handicap 14
Ron Walker, an adult spastic, and the story of his struggle to live a normal life.

2.2 Jack Ashley, MP 16
His work to help the deaf (and other handicapped people).

2.3 The Book of Samuel 18
Sue Maidment and her book about a cat written in hospital during her very serious illness.

2.4 Vic the Chief Engineer 21
The story of Vic, the first woman to win Lloyds Medal for bravery at sea.

2.5   Beauty Is Only Skin Deep   23
A young mother whose hands were badly burned by saving her little boy.

2.6   The Leaf that Never Fell   25
Short story about the artist who painted a leaf on a wall to cheer a sick girl.

2.7   Mousie Thompson   28
Robert Thompson, the woodcarver who used a carved mouse as his trademark.

2.8   Guru Nanak★   31
One of the traditional stories of Nanak, the first of the Sikh Gurus.

2.9   Taroo's Dream★   33
The story of a poor Muslim boy who realized his life's ambition to own a bicycle.

3   HAPPINESS

3.1   Ko-nam and the Dust of Life★   36
Incidents from the story of Liz Thomas who worked in Vietnam with outcasts in Saigon.

3.2   The Circus Clowns   39
Two boys who joined a circus and eventually finished up as partners in a clown act.

3.3   A Boy and His Donkey   42
Pepino, the boy who wanted to take his sick donkey into the crypt of the church in Assisi so that Saint Francis could cure her.

3.4   Terry   48
The Thalidomide baby adopted by two people who were able to bring success and happiness to their own lives for the first time.

3.5   A Pakistani Picnic★   50
A Pakistani girl in England remembers a school picnic at her school in Pakistan.

3.6   Diwali in England★   52
A Kenyan Asian boy makes friends with other coloured boys at his English school through the Diwali festival.

4 COURAGE

4.1 Rescuing the Rescuer 55
A father, trying to rescue his two children in floodwater, is himself swept away and he and his two daughters are rescued by a policeman.

4.2 A Loyal Answer to a Searching Question 57
A young boy struggles to remain loyal to his family without having to lie to hide the truth.

4.3 Don Quixote 60
The old Spanish knight and his attempt to improve the world.

4.4 Nansen and the Fram 62
Nansen's attempt to reach the North Pole by drifting with the ice aboard the *Fram*.

5 SAFETY AND DANGER

5.1 The Bonfire 66
Dramatic story about a bonfire started by three boys near the M62 which led to a multiple car crash.

5.2 Sea Rescue in Hell's Mouth 68
The St Ives' lifeboat rescues five holidaymakers cut off by the tide.

5.3 The Hole in the Ground 72
Two young children in a pot-holing adventure.

5.4 A Corrugated Accident 75
The accident in the steelworks which led to the first production of corrugated sheets.

5.5 Time for Repayment 77
An American boy, rescued from drowning by a woman, nine years later rescues the same woman's husband.

5.6 Saved by an Armband 79
A young boy who didn't bother about road safety is saved by his bright armband.

5.7 Fire 82
Martin Gray and his dedication to protect children in France from forest fires.

5.8 The Three Ds 84
Three boys make a den and start a fire. Each boy reacts quite differently to his punishment.

5.9 No Speak the English★ 86
A Cuban refugee working in the USA and his gallant action in stopping a runaway train loaded with propane.

6 SPORT

6.1 The Man Who Didn't Win 89
Jim Peters and his gallant failure in the Commonwealth Games in Vancouver.

6.2 The Water Champions 91
A boy with polio and his sister who trained so hard they finally represented Australia in the Olympics.

6.3 The Name that Brought a Boy 'Back to Life' 93
Young boy in hospital in a coma is brought back to consciousness by seeing his favourite team on TV in the Cup Final.

6.4 The Girl on the High Trapeze★ 95
An Asian girl in a Children's Home who trained as a circus trapeze artist.

7 THE ENVIRONMENT

7.1 The Blue Whale 99
The story of the blue whale hunted to near extinction and the escape of one baby whale.

7.2 Science Affects All of Us 103
Pollution by man and by animals—DDT and liver fluke.

7.3 Noah and His Ark to the Rescue 106
John Walsh and his work rescuing animals in countries with new hydro-electric dam projects.

7.4 The Butterfly Man 109
Robert Goodden perseveres with his life's work amongst butterflies.

8 MUSIC

8.1 The Gipsy's Violin★ 112
John Dunn, famous violinist, found a Stradivarius owned by an old gipsy. John Dunn hoped to buy the violin but the old man died and the violin was burned with all his possessions.

8.2 Rhythm, Rhyme and Wombles 115
The story of the Wombles of Wimbledon.

8.3   The One-boy Band   117
The boy cornet player who played for the Queen.

9   COMMUNICATION

9.1   Success Story of Perfect Communication   120
Marion Coakes, her perfect understanding with her horse Stroller and their success in the world championship event.

9.2   Joey Deacon—Special Writer   122
Joey Deacon, a spastic, who with the help of three handicapped friends, wrote his autobiography.

9.3   The Story of Tony   125
A slow-learning boy, Tony, who had a strong sense of failure because he seemed to be no good at anything. Then one day, he made a model which was very good . . .

9.4   A Mixture of Nettles and a Fairground Organ★   127
Two Syrian children and their first few days in England.

10   SENSES

10.1   Life with Judy and Daisy (Sight)   131
The story of Esther, a blind woman and her two guide dogs.

10.2   A Lion for the Table (Touch)   133
Antonio Canova's first success as a sculptor with a lion moulded in butter for the Duke's party.

10.3   Jack Ashley, MP (Hearing) see page 16

11   FEAR

11.1   Peter and the Fox   137
Peter had always feared the dark—until his father told how he was taken to a wood when it was dark to see some fox cubs.

11.2   Changing School   140
Nicki was afraid of change and of losing her friends, so when she had to move to a new school, she was really upset—but something happened to help her.

11.3   A Kind Heart and One Tooth Less   143
Old Bishop Aylmer and his sacrifice to help Elizabeth I have a tooth removed without anaesthetic.

12 NEW LIFE

12.1 The Magic of New Life 147
A baby sparrow found by a child was successfully reared and later released.

12.2 The Rose of Peace 149
The story of the famous rose, Peace.

12.3 The Newts that Came to School 151
A teacher who brought newts to school for biology teaching.

13 ANIMALS

13.1 The Elephant Who Didn't Forget 154
Modoc the elephant who remembered her old trainer even though they had not been together for fifty years.

13.2 Follow the Leader 156
Bandoola the elephant leads the great march to safety.

13.3 Corrie the Brave Deer 159
A pet deer who lived with a forest ranger's family in Scotland and defended the baby from the attack of an eagle.

13.4 Zoos Without Bars 161
George Mottershead and his original ideas about natural surroundings for zoos.

14 PETS

14.1 Scruffy 165
A young dog is put out on the streets but finally rescued and cared for by a young girl.

14.2 The Furry Fire Alarm 168
Thanks to the strange visitor a major disaster is avoided.

14.3 Lampo the Railway Dog 170
The stray dog who showed extraordinary skill in travelling by train in Italy.

15 HARVEST

15.1 The Invisible Harvest Festival Gift 173
A boy's hard work at harvest time to cut logs for his grandfather.

15.2 The Mystery of the Harvest Rearranger 175
The harvest produce was rearranged by a mysterious person.

15.3   The Magic of Music★   178
A priest in a remote part of South America had difficulty in getting the villagers to cultivate and harvest the land. He eventually persuaded them with music.

16   CHRISTMAS

16.1   It Really Came True   181
John and Katie help an old lady whose son had disappeared years before. The son returns on Christmas Eve.

16.2   Terry and the Christmas Tree   184
Terry, a young spastic, who wanted his own special Christmas tree. Things went wrong but Terry was able to enjoy his Christmas tree and share it with the people in the town.

16.3   Hughie's Tree   188
How the children brought a happier, merrier Christmas to their austere Scottish village.

16.4   Christmas Was a Baby   190
A baby born near Jerusalem in 1964 and how she came to England.

★ Stories and ideas with a multi-cultural content.

Acknowledgments

For permission to use adaptations to copyright material acknowledgment is made to the following:

For 'Konam and the Dust of Life' from *The Dust of Life* by Liz Thomas to the author and Anthony Sheil Associates Ltd.; for 'Jack Ashley, MP' from *Journey Into Silence* by Jack Ashley and for 'Fire' from *For Those I Loved* by Martin Gray to the authors and The Bodley Head; for 'New Life in the Camp of Death' from *The Miracle on the River Kwai* by Ernest Gordon to the author and Collins Publishers; for 'Lampo the Railway Dog' from *Lampo the Travelling Dog* by Elvio Barlettani to the author and Hutchinson Publishing Group Ltd.; for 'The One-boy Band' from *Over the Hills and Home Again* by Rita Snowden to the author and Methodist Publishing House; for 'The Book of Samuel' from *Samuel* by Sue Maidmont and for 'The Blue Whale' from *Leviathan* by John Gordon Davies to the authors and Michael Joseph Ltd.; for 'Joey Deacon—Special Writer' to the Radio Times; for 'Mousie Thompson' to Robert Thompson's Craftsmen Ltd.

Every effort has been made to trace owners of copyright material, but in some cases this has not proved possible. The publishers would be glad to hear from any further copyright owners of material reproduced in *Primary School Assemblies*.

Introduction

This book is mainly for use with primary/junior children, but can also be used in middle schools and lower secondary schools. The assemblies consist of stories, almost entirely based on true episodes, with a basic theme which young children will be able to understand.

There is a *Prayer/Thought* with every story which the teacher may modify or use as a direct prayer in the traditional manner.

Suggestions for related assemblies, *Assembly ideas*, are given so that one main theme may be followed for a week, or future assemblies on the same theme planned for following weeks. The themes avoid any distinction between religion and life. The assemblies and related activities should involve the pupils (and sometimes parents) in a variety of activities.

Activity and discussion ideas are for the class or group to use to follow up the assembly and thus become part of the normal school programme. This will ensure that the assembly is linked with the children's learning both in school and out. (Many telling points may be made in an assembly but they may be forgotten unless there is some kind of follow-up soon afterwards.)

An example of how an assembly can develop may be taken from 'The bonfire' with the original theme of *Road safety*. The story was based on a brief news item which gave the names of people injured in a multiple car crash when smoke drifted across the M62; it said that police were interviewing some boys who had started a bonfire near the motorway.

In my school, the theme of *Road safety* was used for the week and the police gave talks and the children performed plays to illustrate the theme. After that week, the theme was continued by one class but widened to introduce safety in all its aspects and developed into *Safety and danger*. One of the policemen who had contributed to the *Road safety* week returned to the school and was so impressed by the children's work that he asked for a set of posters for a police exhibition. The posters were put on display in the Hull Central Library, and the children's work was the main part of the exhibition.

1 HELPING OTHERS

1.1 Old George and Lassie

At a school in Grimsby, a girl called Virginia Cooper got up at the end of assembly and stepped on to the platform to appeal to all the children, and the teachers, for help. Virginia was near to tears as she spoke; for her mind was still filled with thoughts of Old George and Lassie.

Old George used to live in a council house, but the house was burned down in a fire soon after George's wife died; so George tramped the streets trying to get lodgings. No one would take him. At every place where he asked, there was always the same reply—'No dogs.'

George said, 'But I promised my dear old wife I would look after Lassie to the end of her days.'

People looked at the old man in his battered old clothes, his long grey overcoat and his old hat. They looked at the fourteen-year-old shaggy dog. They thought of their nice, clean, tidy rooms and said firmly—'No dogs.'

George tried the Salvation Army hostel; but they said the same as the others—'No dogs.'

And every time Lassie just looked sad and wagged her tail slowly; and old George coughed in his tired old way, for he suffered from asthma and bronchitis. The people of Grimsby still saw George and Lassie getting about every day. Each morning, George sat on the same bench in the park sharing a bun or a packet of biscuits with Lassie. Then in the afternoons they tramped round the town, mostly in the shopping arcades. What the people of Grimsby did not know, however, was where George and Lassie spent the night. Virginia saw Old George and Lassie one afternoon as she was hurrying home from school with her aunt.

'Who's that old man with the old dog?' asked Virginia.

'Oh, that's Old George. He's always mooching around here.

He's been living rough ever since his house was burned down.'

'Where does he live now?' asked Virginia.

'Oh, I don't know. Let's get on. We haven't time to think about that old tramp.'

They hurried on; and Old George and Lassie were soon lost in the crowd. Virginia couldn't forget Old George; so she made enquiries about him and found out that he lived in a coalshed. He and the dog had lived there for a year—with no light and no heat, his bed just a pile of blankets in one corner. Then Virginia found out something else: if George didn't get a better place before winter he was certain to get pneumonia and he could die after just one cold night in the coalshed. So that was why Virginia addressed the children and teachers in school assembly.

'We could get some money from a disco,' she said, 'and there will be other things we can do. We could buy Old George a caravan so that he can keep Lassie with him.'

Virginia's appeal reached the newspapers, and in a few days £3000 had been raised; so Old George and Lassie were saved from another winter in the coalshed.

Prayer/Thought
So often a child can see that someone needs help when adults seem blind to that need. May we always try to help anyone who is less fortunate than ourselves.

Assembly ideas
Short plays based on Age Concern and Help the Aged posters and information.

Activity and discussion ideas
Children give one idea for raising money for Shelter or Christian Aid.

Write to Help the Aged and similar national agencies to find ways of helping old people.

Find out about organizations for old folk near the school, e.g. Darby and Joan Clubs, Over 60s, The Salvation Army. Is there anything you can do to help them?

Invite a group of lonely old folk to school for an afternoon's entertainment and tea. Make posters for Help the Aged and send them to Help the Aged, 157 Waterloo Street, London SE1 8UU.

1.2 Last But Not Least

It was the year of the U boat in World War 1 when British merchant ships were being sunk in large numbers by U boats hunting in packs. The convoy of fifty ships was steaming steadily through the Atlantic waters at six knots. For most of the ships, six knots was quite slow; but for No. 048 it was quite fast enough. 048 was a battered old tanker. Everyone else in the convoy hated 048, from the Naval Commander on the bridge of the cruiser escort to the men in lifejackets trying to look calm on board the other oil tankers which would explode at a single shell from a submarine. They all hated 048 because she was the slowest ship and the whole convoy had to travel at the speed of the slowest. Oily, black smoke rose high from the funnel of 048 and everyone thought what a signal that was for any U boat within a thirty kilometre radius. The Commodore called for an increase in speed to eight knots and soon No. 048 lagged behind so that only her smoke could be seen. No one seemed to know the proper name for No. 048. She was a Greek ship and all her crew knew no other language but Greek. The Commodore tried to get messages to the Greek steamer by Aldis signalling lamp; but though the signaller tried again and again (he even attempted semaphore until his arms ached) the only reply was 'No understand'. So that was that.

It was an hour before dawn when the attack started. It was quite dark. Suddenly the lookouts saw a great flash of flame followed by the boom of an explosion. On forty nine ships, horrified watchers saw the bows of the fiftieth, silhouetted in the flames, slide under the water; and then the final explosion as the boilers burst. It was only seconds later when the next ship flared and burned slowly. It was a Canadian ship filled with timber. It burned for a long time and acted as a marker for the U boats.

3

Orders went out from the escort cruiser to increase speed in all ships. In every stokehold, firemen shovelled coal, frantically trying to push up steam pressure. Tired engines of old ships brought out of retirement for the war effort clanked and groaned. Chief engineers swore at the engine-room men and wondered how long the old bearings and worn hull plates could stand the strain. Gun crews stood at the ready at guns sometimes fifty years old because they were all that could be spared for the old ships.

There was another explosion and then another. One moment men were on the bridge; the next, struggling in the icy water trying to reach a raft or piece of wreckage.

The convoy broke course, each ship zigzagging in the hope of disturbing the aim of the torpedo men in the U boats. There were sullen thumps as depth charges were hurled into the water from cruisers and corvettes.

In all, there were seventeen ships sunk before sunrise. When the sun began to lift above the horizon, the U boats withdrew. The cruiser sent corvettes circling around the convoy to count the surviving thirty three ships. Except there were not thirty three. Everybody agreed that there were only thirty two. The Commodore was puzzled. He asked for another check; but still it was thirty two. He sent out an order for the ships to close up. Ships changed course and slowly took up position; but it took some time to line up in the new formation. As they finished the maneuvre, a smudge of oily smoke showed on the horizon as slowly, very slowly, old 048 caught up. And then she received cheer after cheer from the nearest ships; for the decks of 048 were crowded with hundreds of men. Ships in the convoy pulled aside to let her through and 048, belching smoke, struggled through to the front of the convoy. Aboard the cruiser, the Commodore ordered a string of flags to signal to 048 but he guessed that the Greek crew would never read his congratulations. But everyone else knew what 048 had done. She had no speed at all; but she had the guts to stop, with U boats all around her, and rescue an army of drowning men from the icy sea.

Surely, if anything was last but not least, it was old 048?

Prayer/Thought

War is a time when men kill one another: but it is also a time

4

when people show remarkable courage in helping one another. 048 was just an old oil tanker, but on board were men with the courage and compassion to help drowning seamen from other ships in the convoy. We need that kind of spirit today.

Assembly ideas
Aesop's Fables: The hare and the tortoise.
Dunkirk evacuation in World War 2.
Fishermen who followed Jesus.
Famous ships and famous voyages.

Activity and discussion ideas
Make up sea songs, shanties and poems about the sea.
What are some of the worst dangers of the sea?

1.3 New Life in the Camp of Death

The Miracle on the River Kwai was a book written by Ernest Gordon, a prisoner of war of the Japanese in World War 2. There was a film made of the story. The job of building the bridge over the River Kwai was estimated to take five or six years and the Japanese said it had to be done by the prisoners of war in one year. The prisoners worked naked and barefoot in intolerable heat of 49°C. Their bodies were attacked by insects carrying disease; their feet were cut by sharp stones; and all the time, the cruel guards tortured the prisoners. The men collapsed daily and died from thirst, exhaustion, disease and starvation. The chances of survival were slim and it was every man for himself. Prisoners even stole food from each other; and when a prisoner lay dying, the others hung around like jackals waiting for the chance to steal his few possessions so that they could be traded for food.

Then something happened which started a change in the prison camp. It concerned a man called Angus McGillivray, a soldier who was so tough that everyone thought he would be the very last to die. He belonged to the Argylls and it was the tradition for every soldier in the regiment to have one friend to share everything. Angus's friend was seriously ill and everyone knew that he would die; but Angus had decided otherwise. At every mealtime, Angus took food to his sick friend. Then the other soldiers noticed that Angus slipped out of camp late at night. That could only mean the black market: that is, when a prisoner had died, one of the other soldiers would steal the dead man's possessions and creep out at night to sell the things in the village and buy eggs or medicine. Everyone was surprised to see Angus sneaking out at night for he was always thought to be honest and a fine soldier. He never said anything to the others and they never referred to it; but they all thought that Angus was taking his sick friend's few possessions and selling them on the black market. Then, to everyone's surprise, Angus's friend recovered his health; but soon afterwards, Angus collapsed and died. The camp doctor said that he had died of starvation. Then the men realized what Angus had done for his friend.

When the soldiers learned about Angus's sacrifice, the effect was like a miracle. For the very first time they began to help each other. The worst off were the wounded soldiers whose legs had been amputated. Now a cobbler and an engineer designed an artificial leg from odd scraps of wood and metal. They could never hope to make enough legs for all the cripples so they taught the legless to make their own artificial legs. Then some prisoners even organized an orchestra after making many of the instruments themselves. The dead were, for the first time, buried properly, in separate graves—each with the name of the soldier on a wooden cross. Perhaps most important, for the first time hope came to the camp. The prisoners began to see a future and they even began to plan for it.

The war ended. Ernest Gordon and his friends were being moved by train alongside some wounded Japanese soldiers who were without medical care. Some were dying. Ernest Gordon and most of his comrades went over and shared their food and water with the wounded Japanese, although the guards tried to stop them. As the Japanese prison train pulled away, the wounded men shouted, 'Aragatto.' (Thank you.) At the same time, an Allied officer shouted at Ernest Gordon. 'You damned fool. Don't you realize they are the enemy?'

Then Ernest Gordon referred the Allied officer to the story of the Good Samaritan; and he pointed out that it was the prisoners who had suffered most who found it easiest to forgive.

Prayer/Thought
Very often it is people who have experienced suffering who are first to offer help to other people in need.

Assembly ideas
The disciples of Jesus—how they were chosen and how they stood up to difficulties.

Story of Faith, Hope and Charity by Kenneth Poolman (William Kimber 1954), the three old aircraft defending Malta in World War 2.

The inspiration of William Mompesson in the plague village of Eyam (published by the author, Clarence Daniel, at Cratcliffe, Eyam, Nr. Sheffield).

Activity and discussion ideas
The term 'good neighbours' is used in several stories from long ago. What does it mean?

How do you choose a friend? What do you look for?

1.4 Woodbine Willy

'Awake, awake to love and work
The lark is in the sky.'

Those words are the beginning of a hymn known to many school-children. They were written by a remarkable man called Studdert Kennedy. He should be famous, but hardly anyone will know his name. He is still remembered, however, by many old people; but they know him by his strange nickname 'Woodbine Willy'. They would also tell you that Woodbines were popular cigarettes at one time.

Geoffrey Studdert Kennedy was born in a Leeds vicarage. At seven he developed asthma. He was not very handsome; in fact the other boys called him 'Bat ears' and he had huge brown eyes. He was also very absent-minded. He was a dreamer. When he was old enough, he became a teacher for a couple of years; then he went to college to train to be a parson. His first curacy was in Rugby and he went to lodge with a Miss Moore. His landlady soon found that she had to take charge of all her new curate's money because he tended to give it all away to people in need. He even gave away all his clothes to poor people except his cassock (so that he appeared decent). Miss Moore was so sorry for him that she bought him a nice overcoat for the winter. You can guess what Studdert Kennedy did. He gave it away. He had no use for clothes. He loved poor people; and he went to help them— not because he felt he ought, but simply because he wanted to help. Years later, when he was made a royal chaplain, he went to a special gathering in Westminster Abbey in the scarlet robes of a royal chaplain; but underneath, all he wore was a pair of old football shorts.

After some years as a curate, Studdert Kennedy was made vicar of a church in Worcester. His young wife soon found life somewhat difficult. One day she saw her husband taking some bedding out of the house.

'What are you doing with that?' she asked.

'Oh, I'm taking it to an invalid,' said Studdert Kennedy. 'He hasn't any proper bedding.'

Later on, Mrs Studdert Kennedy noticed that pillows were missing; then a mattress disappeared. She guessed what was happening and at first tried to stop her husband giving things away; but finally she helped him carry the bed itself to the poor invalid. And Studdert Kennedy still gave his money away although he now had a wife to support.

When World War 1 began, Studdert Kennedy became an army chaplain and he went to France in December 1915. He used to try and cheer up the British soldiers as they were transported to the trenches. He would sing cheerful songs at the piano in a café. Then he would go to the troop train and give out Woodbine cigarettes and New Testaments from his haversack. That's how he got his name 'Woodbine Willy'.

There were many stories about him. Once an officer was looking for him and he approached a sentry on guard duty.

'Have you seen Captain Kennedy?' asked the officer.

'No, sir.'

'Have you seen the chaplain then?'

'No, sir.'

'Has the padre come this way?'

'No, sir.'

'Look. Have you seen Woodbine Willy lately?'

'Oh yes, sir. He went that way.'

In 1916 Woodbine Willy was posted to the front lines at the Somme offensive. It was a terrible battle and the suffering and killing has been photographed for all to see what a dreadful thing war is. In August 1917 Captain Studdert Kennedy (Woodbine Willy) was awarded the Military Cross for conspicuous gallantry and devotion to duty with great courage while attending the wounded under fire from enemy guns. He searched shell holes for British and German wounded men and brought them into the dressing station for medical attention. His courage and cheerfulness had a remarkable effect on the wounded men; yet Woodbine Willy was a non-combatant.

After the war, Studdert Kennedy went around the country preaching in different churches. He was in Liverpool when he died, probably from overwork and the aftereffect of gas during the war. He was forty five years old. Two thousand people came to the church to pay their respects. They were all there to say goodbye to their comrade and friend. When his coffin was moved to Worcester for burial they found a packet of cigarettes on it. Woodbines, of course.

Prayer/Thought

Let us think of the good work done by people like Studdert Kennedy. These lines of poetry were written by him just before he died:

It is not finished, Lord.
There is not one thing done,
There is no battle of my life,

That I have really won.
And now I come to tell thee
How I fought to fail,
My human, all too human, tale
Of weakness and futility . . .
I cannot read this writing of the years,
My eyes are full of tears,
It gets all blurred, and won't make sense,
It's full of contradictions
Like the scribblings of a child . . .
I can but hand it in, and hope
That Thy great mind, which reads
The writings of so many lives,
Will understand this scrawl
And what it strives
To say—but leaves unsaid.

Assembly ideas

Story of Vincent de Paul when chaplain to the galley slaves.
Children in groups or individually explain 'What friendship
means to me.'

Activity and discussion ideas

Find out some of the facts of World War 1—the numbers of
Allies and Germans killed and injured; the casualties in single
battles.
Do you think that gas, germ and nuclear warfare should be
banned? How can the ban be really effective?
Remembrance Day used to be observed each year at the eleventh
hour of the eleventh day of the eleventh month. Do you think
it was a good idea to remember wars in that way? Would it
help to preserve peace to have a Remembrance Day again?
Some people say that war brings out the worst and the best in
people. Do you think this is true? Find out about other people
who helped others in wartime like Woodbine Willy.

1.5 The X-ray Box

If you looked at a map of the world showing the high land and the low land in different colours, one country would stand out as the highest country in all the world. That country is Tibet. It is covered with mountains, including the Himalayas and Everest. Tibet was always a remote land and the few Europeans who visited it all seemed to agree that the Tibetans were friendly, hospitable, but mysterious. Tibet has great Buddhist monasteries; and there appeared to be more Buddhist monks than ordinary people in the country. For many years, nothing changed in Tibet. Then one day, change did come—with the invasion by Chinese soldiers. Many Tibetans hated the Chinese and they tried to leave the country. Some did get away. To escape from the soldiers they had to cross high mountains, following tracks known only to the local people. It was dangerous and very difficult. Surprisingly, there were thousands of children among the refugees leaving the country. One of them was a boy called Tsering Topygal. He was also called Tsetop (which shortens the first part of each of his names Tsering Topygal). Tsetop was twelve when he followed the Dalai Lama, the Buddhist Tibetan leader, into India. There, Tsetop was taken ill; and everyone was amazed that he had managed the arduous journey over the mountains because he had something wrong with his heart and only a special operation would help him. If he didn't have the operation within a few months he would die; and it could not be done in India because there was no surgeon with the right experience. The nearest hospital for Tsetop's special heart surgery was in Auckland, New Zealand. Members of the Save the Children Fund in New Zealand and Australia raised enough money for Tsetop to fly to Auckland; but there was still the operation to pay for. Tsetop said that he would get the money; and as he spoke he patted his box. Now the box which Tsetop carried was important and it was rather mysterious. He never let anyone else carry it On the sides it said 'X-rays'; but when someone asked if they were X-ray plates Tsetop said, 'No'.

He didn't speak English and all explanations had to be given through a Tibetan interpreter who travelled with Tsetop. That box marked 'X-ray' travelled to the hospital with Tsetop.

'What have you got in that box?' asked the hospital porter. 'Is it some emergency rations in case you don't like our food?'

'Oh no,' said Tsetop through the interpreter, 'nothing like that.'

'Is it a picture of the Dalai Lama?' asked a nurse.

It wasn't.

'I think it is one of those Buddhist prayer messages,' said one of the doctors.

But Tsetop didn't understand what the doctor meant so no one knew whether that guess was correct.

When Tsetop was undressed at the hospital he suddenly handed over his precious box to the interpreter who quickly left the ward before anyone could speak to him. So the X-ray box remained a mystery.

Tsetop's operation was complicated and it lasted five hours. The weary surgeon scrubbed and changed and found a visitor waiting to see him. It was the Tibetan interpreter—quite excited.

'I have got the money,' he said. 'It is all here.'

'What are you talking about?' asked the surgeon.

'We have sold all the pictures for £530,' said the interpreter.

Then he explained that Tsetop's box contained twenty drawings done by Tsetop and other Tibetan children. They were so precious to Tsetop because they were the only way he knew of getting money to pay the hospital and the surgeon.

'Well, you can keep that money,' said the surgeon. 'I am not charging anything; and the hospital will keep Tsetop as a guest— for free.'

When Tsetop heard what the surgeon had said, he decided that the money should be kept and used for another Tibetan child needing special surgery. Tsetop returned to India where the Save the Children Fund ran homes and camps for Tibetan children.

Every year, UNICEF has a World Children's Day when we are asked to remember children in other countries whose standard of living is so much lower than that in our country. What can we do to help?

Prayer/Thought

We think now of suffering children throughout the world. We

think of children in other lands, especially those who are handicapped, hungry or sick; children whose lives are surrounded by war and hatred. Teach us to be grateful for all the nice things that we have; make us unselfish in wanting to make a happier and more hopeful future for children who live in the midst of poverty and despair.

Assembly ideas
Christian Aid suggestions in *Harambee* pamphlet.
Christian Aid suggestions in *Ak Lok* pamphlet.
Children in groups present plays on how our children can help children in other lands.
Speaker from National Children's Homes or local children's home.

Activity and discussion ideas
Is it a good idea to name one day of the year as World Children's Day? Is there a possibility that children's problems will be forgotten for the rest of the year?
Is it enough to collect money to prevent children suffering in other lands? What other things can you do?
Find out what UNICEF means and what it does for children.

2 PEOPLE OF CHARACTER

2.1 Overcoming a Handicap

Ron Walker is handicapped. He is a spastic: that is, his limbs are not properly controlled by the muscles, so he cannot move like a normal person. If you went to see him, he would talk to you about his life and probably give you some typed notes about some of his adventures. He types everything after first talking into his tape recorder. You see, his typing speed is very slow because he has to press the keys down one by one with a little peg. Ron wrote his life story and he starts off with his first days at the school for handicapped children. He went there when he was six. He stayed there until he was sixteen. One cryptic note about his early school days stated, 'Sorry now that I didn't do better.' When he was twelve Ron joined the Scouts. At fifteen, Ron met the Queen at Windsor where he was awarded the Cornell Badge, which is often called the Scout's VC because it is given for outstanding courage and endurance. Ron spent a lot of time with the Scouts, including Scout camp. He travelled around on a three-wheeler trike. Even riding that trike was quite an achievement because, when he had his first trike at eight years of age, Ron couldn't even sit upright. When he was able to sit on the trike, he couldn't get his feet to follow the pedals so his mother tied his feet to the fixed pedals and made Ron push with his legs. It took two years for him to move the trike himself. Years later, with a bigger trike, Ron did the Lyke Wake Walk route in North Yorkshire on his trike with the Scouts. It took him twenty five hours. He had a second go later on, but the going was so bad that the trike broke up and he had to be pulled from the mud and taken home. When he was twenty four Ron decided that his education was not good enough so he went to technical college to take a GCE O-level in English Language. Remember that he could not walk properly and could not use his hands properly. Everything had to be written down by an able-bodied person and Ron had to study for many hours. It took two years but Ron did it and got his certificate.

Ron started a club in Hull called PHAB, which means Physically Handicapped and Able Bodied. He has been to Denmark and France to represent handicapped people. He travels regularly to London. This is how he does it. Ron takes a taxi to the local railway station; then he pushes his walking frame to the train. He travels to the London station. Ron gets out of the train, pushes his walking frame to the taxi rank and so on to his destination—all by himself. It is a remarkable performance for a spastic person; although Ron will never give you the impression that *he* is anything remarkable when he is telling you about his travels. If he is talking to you at his home, most likely, his mother will bring in some cups of tea. The cup will have to be held for Ron because he cannot manage to hold it himself and drink.

Ron loves music and often goes to concerts in the City Hall. He cycles there. Often in the winter it is wet and miserable on the roads but Ron always remains cheerful. Sometimes he falls off his trike, especially when trying to get started in the rain; but he just laughs at himself, climbs on again and sets off for his half-hour ride on the wet roads. He always keeps smiling. Perhaps that is why he got the Scout's VC.

Prayer/Thought
May we, with our own very small handicaps, always remember Ron Walker and battle on, never giving up, and keep cheerful.

Assembly ideas
Get someone from the local physically-handicapped clubs to talk
 about their work with the handicapped.
The story of Helen Keller shows how a remarkable woman
 overcame the handicap of blindness and deafness.

Activity and discussion ideas
What organizations do the group know which help the handicapped? Are they specialist like the Spastics Society? Is it a
 good thing to have an organization to deal with one kind of
 handicap?

Decide on one organization for the handicapped which could be
helped by the school in the present year.

Contact a local club for the handicapped and ask if there is any
way in which the school could help them—maybe by putting
on a concert at the club centre or a display of some kind.

Find out about Thalidomide children and about spina bifida.

2.2 Jack Ashley, MP

Jack Ashley became MP for Stoke-on-Trent and looked like doing
well in Parliament; but he had a little trouble in hearing all the
debates because his left eardrum had been perforated in childhood. Then his right ear became faulty too. A small operation
would soon put his right ear back to normal, he was told. He had
the operation, but his hearing did not improve. He became quite
deaf in both ears. He tried different hearing aids but they were all
quite useless to him. If he continued with his job as MP he knew
that he must learn to lip read in order to follow the debates; so,
instead of attending Parliament, for some time he went to classes
for the deaf in London and practised lip reading for hours every
day. He returned to Parliament to try out his lip reading; but he
couldn't follow any of the speeches. The speakers never seemed
to look his way long enough for Jack to read their lip movements.
At break time, Jack went to the bar where his friends gave him a
good welcome. One old friend asked Jack something. Jack
stared and saw that his friend was saying something again. From
the movement of his friend's lips, Jack could tell that he was
shouting. Jack felt cold fear, for he could hear nothing, and he
had no idea what his friend had said. He could not lip read one
single word—and this with a friend speaking slowly and directly
in front of him. What chance did he have in Parliament where
the speakers would be far away and talking in a normal voice?
Jack went home to write out his resignation. His wife, Pauline,
was very upset because she knew how hard Jack had worked to
overcome his handicap and how he loved the work of Parliament. She wrote out a message to Jack to try and dissuade him.

When she carried on writing about the disabled people and how Jack could help them as MP, Jack changed his mind about resigning and decided to try again.

Some time afterwards, Jack was asked to introduce a Bill in Parliament setting up a commission to look into the problems of disabled people. Jack was very excited by the prospect but also frightened because he had not done any public speaking since his total deafness; and now, of course, he could not hear his own voice; and he had no idea whether he was speaking quietly or shouting. The weekend before Jack was due to make his speech, he attended a large meeting of disabled people in Trafalgar Square. There were hundreds of people in wheelchairs from all over Britain. What impressed Jack was the cheerfulness and courage of those crippled people. It gave him strength and confidence to speak on their behalf in the Commons. Jack made his speech to a full house in Parliament. Even members of the Opposition were there to listen to him with sympathy and respect, as he told them about the meeting he had attended in Trafalgar Square. As he sat down he could feel the cheering which he couldn't hear and the Prime Minister touched his arm and said just three words which he managed to lip read. 'Well done, Jack.'

You may have heard Jack Ashley on the radio or television. Like all deaf people, he has a strange voice because he cannot hear anything he says even if he shouts; but he speaks so well that anyone could understand what he says. His devotion to the well-being of disabled people and particularly his work for deaf people has resulted in at least two inventions specially for the deaf. One is a machine for transmitting phonetic shorthand, which was an original idea of Jack Ashley's and developed by Southampton University. The very first message on the machine said:

THIS E QUIP MNT WIL FUR ST
BEE UE SD IN T HOUS OF CO MONS
THIS AF TUR NOON. FEB WUN
BIE MR JAC ASH LI, MP

Another idea just put into use is a telephone linked to a teleprinter so that deaf people can send typed messages by phone with a special machine.

If Jack Ashley had given up when total deafness cut him off from the other MPs in Parliament, perhaps those wonderful aids for deaf people would never have been invented.

Prayer/Thought

There may be many other people like Jack Ashley who will try to help the cause of the handicapped. May their work prosper so that happiness is spread; and may we be thankful that we can do so many things without a handicap.

Assembly ideas

The senses taken separately.

Set up a court of enquiry to look at evidence for/against a new gipsy site nearby.

Stories of deaf people—Beethoven, Helen Keller.

Jesus and the deaf and dumb man.

Story of the telephone.

Activity and discussion ideas

One of the latest ideas of an aid for deaf people is to use a pet dog. How can such an animal be trained to help a deaf person?

How useful are our ears when other senses are not in use? Try listening (with eyes closed) to identify sounds of paper tearing, water pouring, doors closing etc.

Are present-day noise volumes too high for safety? It has been suggested that children's hearing may be damaged by music played too loud at discos.

2.3 The Book of Samuel

Many children and parents like Spike Milligan's books. His name is on one book which is all about cats; but Spike didn't write it—he helped to get it printed. The book was written by a girl called Sue Maidment. Spike Milligan wrote an introduction to the book.

The book is the story of Samuel the Spanish cat and his adventures in Scotland. Samuel's parents, grandparents and great-great-grandparents are all shown on a special drawing called a family tree. It took Sue Maidment quite a long time to write the stories about Samuel and his friends. (There are several stories in the book.) She spent hours and hours just thinking out stories about animals—particularly cats. Can you think why a schoolgirl should take a long time to write a story? She couldn't hold a pen or pencil without pain. The stories of Samuel were actually typed out on Sue's small pink typewriter.

When Sue was five years old she was given her first kitten called Twinkle when she came out of hospital. She had something wrong with her kidneys. Twinkle slept on Sue's bed every night. She loved animals; but cats were always her favourites. In her bedroom she had a doll's house; but she didn't keep dolls in it—she filled it with toy mice and called it Mouse House. The walls of her room were covered with pictures of cats. When Sue was eleven, her father died and soon afterwards Sue became ill. She was too ill to go to school; and her doctors decided that she would need an operation so that she could be connected to a kidney machine. Her mother told her the truth—that Sue had a chronic kidney disease.

When Sue came home from hospital, her mother gave her another kitten which she called Tuppence. Sue had to take lots of tablets for blood pressure and she had to stay on a strict diet which meant no biscuits or cakes or chocolate or ice cream. So many of the things she liked she was not allowed to eat. Perhaps that is why there is so much about food in her story of Samuel. Yet everyone says that Sue was nearly always cheerful. She thought out stories and usually tape recorded them until she could get on with the typing. By the time Sue was twelve she was in terrible pain. Her hands were bent and misshapen. She used to sit with her knees clutched under her chin. She could only move with crutches. Then she needed a wheelchair to get around. She never gave up trying to live as normal a life as possible and would never be treated as an invalid. She played wheelchair tennis by knocking a ball tied to a long string which could travel along a fixed clothes line in the garden; and every day she would tap, tap, tap on her little pink typewriter with Twinkle watching her on the next chair. Sometimes there were two other cats watching too. They were called Bo and Peep and were brought in by friends. Bo and Peep were the inspiration for the two Siamese cats in the Samuel book. By this time, Sue was working on stories about Samuel. And just at this time she had an obsession—a fixed idea which filled her mind and wouldn't go away. Her obsession was a date—August 15th. She thought something would happen to her on that day. No one ever found out what was in Sue's mind. The psychiatrist at the hospital tried to persuade Sue that perhaps August 15th would be the day when she could have a kidney transplant. They put a circle round that day on her calendar and they tried to make it a date for something nice to happen. Sue worked harder and harder on her book. She seemed to be racing against time; and everyone could see that she was trying to finish it before August 15th. She did. On August 14th Sue had a check up. She stayed in bed all day long now in the hospital; and she knew that she could live only a short time if a suitable kidney transplant could not be found. August 15th dawned and dragged on. Even the nurses were quite subdued and couldn't make their little jokes to get Sue smiling. The day passed—and nothing happened.

Six months later, Sue had her transplant operation. The new kidney started working and within one week, Sue was having physiotherapy to get her on her feet and moving again. Then on the Bank Holiday weekend there was a relapse. She died.

Sue's mother wrote to Spike Milligan to try and get his help with Sue's book. Spike wrote the introduction to Samuel and helped to get it published. Sue's mother said that all the royalties, which usually go to the author, would be given to a special hospital to help people suffering from kidney disease.

Prayer/Thought
May we be inspired by the simple faith and courage of Sue Maidment; and may our courage never fail even when things seem hopeless.

Assembly ideas

The Chloroform Man, *The Policeman*, *The Penicillin Man*, *The Insulin Man* by Rowland (Lutterworth Press).

The story of Rahere the court jester who wanted to build a hospital (St Bartholomew's), *Me* by G. Mattock (Oliver and Boyd).

Accidents, diseases, operations, nurses, doctors, scientists.

Activity and discussion ideas

Find out about treatment for people with diseased kidneys—machines and transplants.

Discuss what are the most important things in life.

What should we do to enjoy good health?

2.4 Vic the Chief Engineer

You may have heard grown-ups talking about an Act of Parliament which tries to ensure that women will have the chance to apply for all kinds of jobs which used to be done by men. The Act also applies to other areas where there was discrimination. On television there was a news item about a public house where two men and two women were being interviewed. Nothing special in that—except that the interview took place in the men's bar from which women had always been banned. The two women were the first to challenge the idea of a bar exclusively for men.

If you took a car to be mended in a garage, it is most likely that the mechanic would be a man. The crew of a merchant ship would be unlikely to include women. There would be a few women working on some big ships; but you would expect the ship's engineer to be a man; and the captain would be a man on most of our British ships.

This is the story of a ship's engineer called Vic.

Vic had always wanted to go to sea and worked through all the engine-room jobs as second engineer on merchant ships. Then, after passing examinations and going on many trips on several boats, Vic became a chief engineer and continued in that job for many years. Then, at forty years of age, Vic decided to retire and take a shore job. Vic said, 'I don't ever want to set foot on a boat again—unless it is as a passenger.'

But World War 2 started in that same year; and of course, one of the first volunteers to go back to sea was Vic.

Vic's ship was used in the Dunkirk evacuation, making six separate Channel crossings with exhausted and wounded British soldiers, under constant attack from German bombers. It was an experience which prepared Vic for the toughest voyage of her life. '*Her* life' because, you see, Vic was a woman. Her full name was Victoria Drummond. She was the first woman in the world to hold a chief engineer's ticket.

It was in 1941 that attacks on British merchant shipping became so heavy that even Winston Churchill was worried. Vic's ship was crossing from America when it was spotted by a German Condor. The German plane flew at low level and dropped the first salvo of bombs right on target. In the engine-room Vic was blown off her feet by the blast. She staggered up, bruised and badly shaken, but she realized at once that the only hope for the ship was to steer a zigzag course at increased speed. The ship had a normal speed of just nine knots. Vic increased pressure in the boilers and pushed the speed up to nearly thirteen knots. Now the Condor had returned for a second run over the ship. Vic felt the shock of bombs and never really knew they were near misses until she heard the engine-room men give a cheer. She was so busy concentrating on keeping up the speed that she never had time to think of the German Condor returning to the attack. Then came the third run. The stick of bombs was right on target and the engine-room filled with scalding steam from a fractured pipe-jet. Vic ordered all the engine-room men on deck. At first they refused to leave her. 'I'll have you all on a charge of mutiny,' she shouted. 'Get up on deck.'

For the next forty five minutes Vic wrestled alone with controls in the engine-room. She could hardly see for steam; and oil dripped on her face from broken pipes. Again and again the Condor came in to attack until all its bombs were gone; but Vic knew there was no all clear for her with boilers threatening to explode at any moment. She brought down the pressure when the ship's speed was reduced; and then one of Vic's engine-room staff came down to help. Vic slowly climbed the steel ladder out of the engine-room and for the first time was able to relax.

The ship got back to England and later on, Vic went to Buckingham Palace to be awarded the MBE and Lloyd's War Medal for bravery at sea—the first woman ever to win that award.

Prayer/Thought
Girls can be as brave as boys. Many women have risked their lives when friends and comrades were in danger. Boys and girls can help anyone in danger and they can help each other.

Assembly ideas
Famous women of character—Elizabeth Fry, Florence Nightingale, Amy Johnson, Sue Ryder.
The first Victoria Cross awarded to Charles Lucas.
The sea—fishermen and sailors.

Activity and discussion ideas
Are girls interested in engineering jobs nowadays?
Why should most sailors be men?
Are girls more suited to some jobs and boys fitted for others?

2.5 Beauty Is Only Skin Deep

Have you ever noticed that there are some things we never appreciate until they are not there? Sometimes we take people for granted. The day one mother went into hospital, the young daughter tried to cook for her father and her young brother. Unfortunately she put everything in to cook at the same time. The meat was not done, the potatoes boiled dry and the dinner was ruined. The small brother offered to do the washing; but he put all the clothes into the washing machine and all the colours ran, making a horrible mess of his sister's dress and his father's best shirt. They both thought it was easy because, week in week out, they had seen mother doing the cooking and washing and they never appreciated that the work was not as easy as it looked. Things with which we are familiar we take for granted. We rarely appreciate the good things around us until they are not there. We rarely look closely at familiar things. It may be that children never really know their parents as people; and it may be that someone outside the family says: 'He is such a nice, kind man' and it is a surprise to realize that 'he' happens to be your own father; or perhaps a neighbour says: 'She is such a generous, helpful woman' and she means your own mother.

Richard was one of those happy children who made friends easily; so when his family moved to a new house, Richard quickly made friends with several boys in his new school. He played with his friends after school in the bit of woodland left near the house where he lived. Sometimes the boys played in one of their gardens; and on some evenings they watched television together. Richard always liked it best when he could bring his friends home to tea.

When Richard was about ten, his father noticed that the other boys no longer came to tea in their house. Sometimes they played in the garden but they hardly ever came in the house.

Richard's father wondered what was wrong. 'What happened to John and Michael who used to come to tea so often?' he asked.

'Oh, they are all right,' said Richard.

'Why don't they come to tea then like they used to?'

'Oh, I don't know,' said Richard.

Richard's father could see that his son was embarrassed by something and he guessed what it was.

'Is it because of your mother's hands?' asked Richard's father. 'I can see that it is.'

Then he told Richard about how his mother had been such a beautiful woman with a lovely skin and hands. Before Richard was born she had been a demonstrator of make-up for a famous company selling cosmetics. She gave up her job to look after her baby boy Richard. One day, when Richard was two, she heard him screaming from another room. She rushed to him and found him with his clothes alight near the fire. She tore off the burning clothes with her bare hands, her beautiful hands. Then she carried her screaming little boy to the bathroom and ran cold water over him to cool his skin. He went to hospital and stayed there for a week; but he had no serious burns and so he came home. But Richard's mother had to stay longer in hospital. Her hands were badly burned and skin grafts were made to repair some of the damaged flesh. The grafts were not all successful, so that her hands healed with all the scars showing and some of her fingers were not quite straight. She had saved Richard; but she had sacrificed her hands.

Richard listened intently to every word of his father's story. He never said anything; but next day, he brought two friends home—John and Michael. Before they came into the house, Richard said to them: 'Look at my mother's hands when you go in. She burnt them because she loved me.'

Prayer/Thought
Sometimes we should try to look at people in our own family and think how much we owe them and how little we appreciate them. We should remember to say 'Thank you' for those every-day things which we often take for granted.

Assembly ideas
Hands—using our hands (craftsmen)
        touch (blind)
        language of hands (deaf and dumb)
        clever hands (musicians)
        hands showing suffering (artists)
        helping hands (doctors, nurses).

Activity and discussion ideas
Design a machine or some tools which can be used in the kitchen or garden by people who are manually handicapped.

2.6 The Leaf that Never Fell

Every year, some people look forward to autumn because they say that the colours of the trees and plants are at their most beautiful. Many people try to visit the moors, the lakes or the forests just to enjoy the sight of the rich browns, reds and yellows of the autumn colours. Other people are not so happy about autumn because it is the season before winter; and they don't like the idea of cold weather coming. In New York, the winters are very bleak and far colder than the weather we expect in England.

Two young women, Sue and Joanne, were sharing a flat in New York one autumn. They were both artists. They worked for an advertising firm making posters and pictures for magazines. Then Joanne became ill and had to stay in bed. The doctor said that Joanne was very seriously ill with pneumonia and she would have to be watched and cared for day and night. Sue said that she would bring some work to do at home and would look after Joanne. Two days later Joanne looked worse and when the doctor saw her he told Sue that the pneumonia had weakened her friend so much that she had lost the will to live. People as sick as Joanne had to be determined to get better. Joanne seemed to be just lying in bed waiting to die. Sue returned to the bedroom. Joanne appeared to be wandering in her mind. She was counting aloud.

'Twelve and then eleven.'

Then Joanne stared out of the window at the wall of the flats next door.

'What are you saying?' asked Sue.

'I'm counting the last leaves on the vine on that wall. The leaves are dying just like me. When the last leaf falls dead I shall die too.'

'Don't be silly,' said Sue.

But Sue was very worried and she wondered what to do. Later, when she went out to get some more medicine for Joanne, Sue met an old friend. It was Mr Behrman, an old artist who lived in the flat below the girls'. Sue told Mr Behrman about Joanne's serious illness and her obsession with the dying vine leaves.

'I wish I could do something to help,' Mr Behrman said sadly, 'but I'm too old to be of much use.'

Later on, the old artist looked out of his window and he could just see the remaining leaves on the vine creeper—there were six left. But would they stay much longer? The old man sighed. All his life he had wanted to paint pictures. When he was a young man he had thought that one day he would be famous; but his paintings never sold for more than a few dollars, and in fact, he just managed to earn enough for his rent and food. He couldn't help that sick girl with money, for he hadn't any to spare.

Next morning Joanne's first words were: 'Sue, pull back the curtains and let me see.'

Sue did as she was told and looked out herself. There was just one leaf left on the vine.

'When that leaf goes, that will be the end for me,' said Joanne.

Sue didn't know what to say. The day dragged on miserably. It was raining outside and the daylight faded quickly in the late afternoon. Sue drew the curtains and thought about the last vine leaf. It was still there, fluttering in a slight breeze; but she was sure it would fall that night. She looked at Joanne's pale face on the pillow and a slow tear ran down Sue's cheek. Next morning, Joanne's first words as usual were: 'Sue, draw back the curtains.'

She hesitated. She prayed that the leaf would still be there. Then she slowly pulled back the curtains and looked out. The vine leaf was still there. The day passed somehow, with Sue looking out of the window many times even though she tried not to. The leaf stayed in place all day.

Next morning, after Joanne's usual request, Sue opened the curtains. The leaf was still there. Joanne looked out for quite a long time. Then she said: 'I think that leaf has stayed there specially for me. There is something strange about it. It's a kind of prophecy saying I shall live. I don't want to die, Sue. I'll eat a little soup right now.'

Sue was delighted. She knew that her friend was now past the worst and would get stronger. Several days later, Joanne was strong enough to get up and sit in a chair near the window.

'Look, Sue,' she said. 'That leaf is still there; and think how it has stayed on the vine through all those terrible winds we have just had.'

'I have something to tell you,' said Sue. 'Mr Behrman died in hospital today. They found him unconscious in his room five days ago, blue with cold and fully dressed. He had a torch in one hand and his painting palette in the other. Can you guess what he had been doing?'

'He painted the leaf,' said Joanne.

'Yes,' said Sue. 'It was the greatest work of his life; and he did it to save your life.'

Prayer/Thought
We can all learn from the good example of Sue and the sacrifice of kind old Mr Behrman, who probably thought himself to be a failure. Yet the artist's last painting, a very simple picture, was priceless—it helped to save a life.

Assembly ideas
The Good Samaritan.
Captain Oates's sacrifice in the Antarctic.
Father Damien and the lepers by John Farrow (Burnt Oates).

Activity and discussion ideas
Read the words of 'When I needed a neighbour' by Sydney
  Carter, *Songs for the Seventies*, Galliard, 1971. What are your
  views? Who is my neighbour? What makes a good neighbour?

2.7 Mousie Thompson

The year 1976 was the hundredth anniversary of the invention of the telephone by Graham Bell. In 1876 there were many other famous inventions. We tend to remember major events like that; and a few people, especially kings and queens, politicians, inventors, scientists and explorers, become so well known that their names are written in history books and they are remembered for a long time. Ordinary people are not often mentioned in history so they are forgotten unless something permanent from their life is left behind when they die. Fortunately, history is not just something written in books. It is all around us. Everything you see has a history. If you were really interested in the history of, say, Yorkshire, you could learn a lot from just one village. One village in Yorkshire is called Kilburn. It is so tiny that it is difficult to find on a map. Very few people have heard of Kilburn; but if you went there you would notice something about the place as soon as you got near it. On the hill backing onto the village is a huge carving in the chalk. It is in the shape of a horse— the Kilburn horse. In the village at weekends, you would most likely have difficulty in parking a car because the place is full of visitors. Yet the visitors may not bother to climb the hill to the white horse; they have come to see something quite different— the local carving business of Thompsons.

In that village of Kilburn, Robert Thompson was born in 1876, the year when Bell invented the telephone. Robert Thompson was a very ordinary man. His father was the village joiner, and Robert, when he was old enough, helped his father making carts and gates in the workshop. Robert was a good joiner. He had a feeling for wood, and when he had finished his work for the day he still worked in wood, but this time just for his own pleasure. Robert was fascinated by wood carving. He wanted to be a wood carver like the craftsmen of the fifteenth and sixteenth centuries. One day, he was working with his friend Charlie Barker in a church. They were fitting a new beam and Charlie said: 'Do you know, I think we are as poor as church mice.'

Robert said nothing, but he carried on carving something on the beam.

'Did you hear what I said, Robert?' said Charlie, as he turned to look at his friend.

Then Charlie laughed because he could see that Robert had heard. On the beam was carved a tiny mouse. When they finished work for the day, Robert forgot about the mouse. Later on, Robert Thompson began to get orders for carving in wood. He made a large cross for the cemetery at Ampleforth. Then he did a lot of work for Ampleforth College. If you are ever able to go there you can still see his wood carving in the library and the choir stalls. People began to ask Robert to make furniture. It was at that time that he began to think he should mark his work in some way. The idea came to him to use the little creature he often saw near his store of oak: a mouse. He thought of himself as mouse-like. He thought of how a mouse manages to scrape and chew away the hardest wood with its chisel-like teeth; and how the mouse works quietly with nobody taking notice. He thought that was like his workshop hidden in the country. It was what Robert Thompson called 'industry in quiet places'.

So, on all his work, Robert Thompson carved a little mouse; and people began to call him Mousie Thompson and forgot the Robert part of his name. The early mouse mark of Thompson was lifelike with fully-carved front legs; but, later on, Thompson made a different shape, streamlining the mouse so that the front legs hardly showed.

Mousie Thompson used to say: 'My work will last a thousand years.'

His hand-carved furniture went to houses and churches all over the world, and on every piece, if you searched well, you would see a little mouse—perhaps running up the leg of a table or under a chair seat. In Westminster Abbey there is the little mouse on the carved candlesticks and in York Minster the Archbishop sits on his throne and the little mouse is there too. Even public houses have mouse furniture. So if you ever see some well-carved, heavy oak furniture, have a good look at it and see if you can spot Mousie Thompson's trademark.

Robert Thompson's cottage and workshop are still there under the white horse at Kilburn. Now there is a large wood-working business carried on by Mousie's grandsons. It is still hand-carving and you can see the men working in the work-shops. It is a popular place; so that's why it is so difficult to park a car in the tiny village of Kilburn.

Prayer/Thought

It is a good thing to take a pride in our work, to do our best to improve our skills and to set ourselves high standards. Mousie Thompson never found his work boring; he was always in-terested and happy in his work.

Assembly ideas

Working hands—blacksmith, joiner, potter, cook, farmer, typist, dressmaker, mechanic.

Story of Michelangelo's sculpture of David.

Bad craftsmanship nearly ended the life of Dr Grenfell because a young craftsman in England had put one steel screw in the case of a new compass for the doctor who, later on, lost his way in Labrador and nearly perished.

Activity and discussion ideas
How do our hands differ from those of most mammals?
Are there any craftsmen working near the school? What kind of craftsmen are they?

2.8 Guru Nanak

In the Sikh religion, great men are given the title of Guru. The first of the Sikh Gurus was born in Nankana, Pakistan, some five hundred years ago. His name was Nanak. There are many stories of Nanak and his adventures. When he was sixteen, Nanak had many friends; and two of the closest were Bala, a Hindu, and Mardana, a Muslim. Nanak's father didn't like the idea of his son having a Muslim friend and a Hindu friend.

'When we are together, Bala and Mardana are my brothers,' said Nanak. 'We forget about Hindu and Muslim.'

Nanak used to say that all men were brothers in one big family. His father was often angry with Nanak because the boy so often gave things away. Nanak gave away his clothes, books, money— even his food to poor boys in the village. His father used to shout at him:

'Why do you give everything away? I have worked hard to give you a good start in life; and all you do is laze about and give things to other children. We shall have to find some work for you to do.'

Nanak's father wanted his son to earn a lot of money so that he could live in a big house with many servants to wait on him. Nanak was given twenty rupees (worth a lot of money in those days) and told by his father to go to the city and trade (that is to buy and sell at a profit) then return home.

Nanak set out with his friends Bala and Mardana walking towards the city. In every village they passed through they talked to the people telling them to live as one family helping one another. When they reached the jungle they came across a group of twenty men who seemed to spend most of their day praying to God. They were holy men. They all looked very thin and weak. Nanak and his friends stayed with the holy men. Nanak soon found out that the men never had enough to eat. He thought about his own words of wisdom to the villagers on the journey when he had told them to help everyone and love everyone. They were fine words, but only words. As he thought about the twenty holy men his fingers closed on the twenty coins he still carried. Suddenly he said to his friends:

'Let's go out and buy food for our hungry brothers.'

So Nanak, Bala and Mardana spent the twenty rupees on food which they took to the holy men. Then all three returned to their own village. Nanak's father was delighted to see his son back.

'How did you get on with trade?' asked his father.

'I did well,' said Nanak.

'How much did you make?'

'Nothing at all,' said Nanak.

Nanak's father asked his son to repeat his words because he thought he had misheard.

When Nanak's father asked his son to explain, Nanak told him that he had made the best trade possible by feeding twenty hungry men. When he heard that, Nanak's father was very angry and he hit Nanak. Nanak stood still and was quiet for a minute. Then he said:

'Father, you don't understand! One day you will!'

Prayer/Thought

Many religious teachers say the same kind of things—often to remind people that we all belong to one family. Peace between people is only possible if we remember that we are all neighbours.

Assembly ideas

Other incidents from the story of Guru Nanak.

Invite a member of the Sikh community to talk about Sikhism.

Children demonstrate the five 'Ks' of Sikhism: Kangha—comb; Kesh—untrimmed hair; Kirpan—sword; Kara—iron bangle; Kachs—short undertrousers.

Activity and discussion ideas
Why did Nanak give away all his father's money?
Sikh motor cyclists in Britain wanted to keep their turbans as
    protection when crash helmets were made compulsory. What
    do you think of this?
Sikhs working on buses also wanted to wear their turbans in-
    stead of the uniform cap which everyone else had to wear.
    What do you think?
What are the advantages of wearing a uniform at school?
What people wear uniform and why?

2.9 Taroo's Dream

If you had asked Taroo what he was thinking when he had that
far-away look he would answer—always in the same sing-song
voice:

'I am thinking of a bicycle—a bicycle that I can ride away to
Shalimar to see the Moghul Gardens or to the Emperor's tomb
in Shahdara. I could ride through the town so fast that no one
could catch me.'

Taroo's thoughts were nearly always about a bicycle; but
there was little hope that he would ever own one. The family was
very poor and he had many brothers and sisters. His father,
Budhu, was a street sweeper in Lahore; and Taroo helped him to
sweep the streets and collect horse manure to sell for a little extra
money. When Taroo was fourteen he decided to try his luck as a
cha-wallah, selling tea in cracked cups on the side of a busy road
going through Lahore. It was dusty, noisy and hot. Not an ideal
place for a street café; but the bad conditions made everyone
thirsty and Taroo had a happy smile which somehow brought
him plenty of custom in the daytime. Even after nightfall there
were regular customers who liked the friendly light of his pressure lantern.

It was one of the regular customers who told Taroo about the
job in the bicycle shop. The owner, Mohammed Ashraf, wanted
a boy to train as an apprentice and learn the trade of cycle re-
pairer. Taroo went to see Mohammed Ashraf and in less than

five minutes he had convinced the owner that only one boy in all Lahore could fit that job—Taroo, of course.

It was a dirty, oily job but Taroo loved it. Even if he could never afford to buy a bicycle, at least he could work with them. He learned the trade very quickly and Mohammed Ashraf was soon able to leave the shop with Taroo in charge.

One day, Mohammed Ashraf went out to buy his rations of wheat and sugar and he left Taroo in charge of the cycle shop. Soon after his employer had gone, a customer brought a cycle which he wanted repaired immediately. The bicycle didn't take very long to put right, but even in those few minutes the customer seemed unusually impatient and nervous. He was talking quietly to his companion and Taroo heard just a few words now and again. He heard the police mentioned, then something about the 14.30 plane to Dacca next day. The word 'gold' was mentioned twice and what sounded like 'well hidden'. After they had gone, Taroo thought about the conversation—especially the gold. He knew that gold smuggling was commonplace and smugglers were always in the news. Could his recent customer be a gold smuggler?

When Mohammed Ashraf returned, Taroo told him about his suspicions.

'You must come with me to the police and tell them,' said Mohammed Ashraf.

So Taroo told his story to the police. Two days later, Taroo was listening to the local radio in his favourite café when he heard an announcement that one of the planes (the 14.30 flight) to Dacca had been recalled the previous day and the luggage of two of the passengers had been searched. 1,500 tolas of gold had been found well hidden in one of the cases.

One month later, when Taroo had nearly forgotten the affair, the police sent for him and they gave him a reward for information leading to the arrest of the gold smugglers. The reward was 250 rupees—just enough to buy a new Rustum, the bicycle he had seen in his dreams.

Prayer/Thought

Dreams can come true—especially if we do something to help them.

Assembly ideas

Other countries. Information from travel agents. Children who have travelled in other countries.

One world. To make people more aware of the need for overseas development.

Occupations—ancient and modern, e.g. blacksmith, computer programmer.

Activity and discussion ideas

Many people in Taroo's country are Muslims. Find out which other countries in the world are mostly Muslim. How does this religion differ from Christianity? Are there any similarities?

Taroo started work earlier than a child is allowed to do in Britain. What are the rules about the employment of schoolchildren (including paper delivery) in Britain?

Compare what you enjoy most in your life in the United Kingdom with what you might enjoy in Taroo's life.

3 HAPPINESS

3.1 Ko-nam and the Dust of Life

When Ko-nam visited the hospital, all the patients were pleased to see her. With her blonde hair, she was easy to spot in that hospital; for Ko-nam was English and she was working in a hospital in Saigon, Vietnam—full, at that time, with communist soldiers. The war had ended and Ko-nam had made up her mind to stay in Vietnam to help as many people as she could. She was a trained nurse, much needed at that time; but the North Vietnamese troops occupying Saigon had threatened to chop off the heads of any Americans they found in the city; and Ko-nam had blonde hair like the Americans. At first, Ko-nam kept her hair covered with a head scarf; then she dyed it black. Unfortunately, it didn't look natural and the soldiers all knew that Ko-nam was foreign; but they didn't trouble her. The hospital was so full of wounded men that some of the patients were left on stretchers in the corridors. Ko-nam came to see one young lad, about her own age, lying on a stretcher. His head was swathed in bandages saturated in blood; so Ko-nam gently unwrapped one eye—but there was no eye there, only blood and bits of flesh. The soldier was in terrible pain so Ko-nam got him to another hospital where he could be properly treated. Ko-nam was a volunteer nurse in that hospital. She often stayed there all evening because all the doctors and regular nurses left at 4.30 p.m. each day and didn't come back until next morning.

Every day in Saigon was a day of danger for Ko-nam because she was never certain whether the North Vietnamese soldiers would take her away as a suspected spy merely because she spoke English. In fact, she was never locked up; but she was told to report for indoctrination where she was lectured in communist theory, and the North Vietnamese tried to get Ko-nam to be a follower of Ho-Chi-Min, the communist leader. Ko-nam said she never understood what they were talking about. She told the communists that she believed in two things: giving love and receiving love. The communists couldn't argue about that because they knew that Ko-nam had been giving love to the outcasts of Saigon for three years during the terrible war. She really cared for people; and the ones she looked after included drug addicts, prostitutes and homeless children. Ko-nam's English name was Liz Thomas. The Vietnamese couldn't say her name properly so when Liz told them she was the fifth child in her family in London, her Vietnamese friends called her Ko-nam, which means 'Girl number 5'.

Liz had wanted to go to Vietnam ever since she was fourteen and heard, at school, about the plight of the Vietnamese children; but she was twenty, a trained nurse, before she had her chance. To most people who knew her, Liz Thomas was a very ordinary girl; but she had persistence—she knew what she wanted to do and she was determined to do it. In Saigon, she soon found it wasn't a nurse they needed: it was someone to care for them—to give them love. Children without homes lived in the streets and drifted from place to place just getting enough food to live. The children called themselves 'The dust of life' because they were like the dust in the hot streets blowing everywhere. Later on, Liz wrote a book about her experiences and she gave it the title *The Dust of Life* in memory of her Saigon children—the ones she cared for. The authorities in Saigon decided to clean up the city and all the homeless people were put in a centre which was really a prison. The children were mixed in with adults from other families—some of them criminals. Liz fetched many children out of the centre and looked after them in the house where she lived. She got a dog for the children to play with. They all loved dogs and they called this one Nixon. Every child wanted to sleep next to Nixon so they had to make a rota and Nixon slept in a different place each night. Then one day, Nixon died. The children made a coffin out of an old box and they wanted to give their pet a proper funeral. They went outside and began to dig a grave. Suddenly the diggers were surrounded by police. The grave was just outside the police station and the police thought that the children were putting a bomb in the ground to blow up the police station. They refused to let the children bury Nixon there so they had to find another spot.

After the communists took over Saigon, Liz found it more and more difficult staying there. She and the children lived for day after day on just plain rice and vegetable soup—no meat, fish, cheese, milk or tea, no bread and butter—just rice and soup. Even so, Liz tried to help young people in distress. She went frequently to the drug-addict area—the only European who could go there without fear of attack. Liz would help anyone, no matter what they had done; and all the people trusted her. But one day, a teenage girl Liz had once helped came to the house to talk to Liz. After the girl had gone, the radio was missing and Liz knew that the girl had stolen it. It was serious because the radio was something which could be sold for food; it was as good as money. A few days later, a thief took all Liz's money. It was the end for the children and their home with Liz. All their remaining possessions were shared out and all the children left the home— some to go to friends and others to drift again as 'The dust of life'.

Liz cried when they left but, as she said, at least when they were together they had a little happiness. They would remember. It had all been worthwhile.

Prayer/Thought
We thank God for ordinary people like Liz, known as Ko-nam, who spread love and happiness in a hostile world.

Assembly ideas
The story of Kagawa and his work in Japan's shanty towns will give many ideas for other assemblies (*Toyohiko Kagawa* by C. M. Simon, published by Hodder and Stoughton).

Instances of selfless devotion to the homeless and poor can be found in the lives of people like Father Borrelli, Gladys Aylward, Dr Barnardo (*Heroes of our Time* published by Gollancz 1967).

Activity and discussion ideas
Some people say it is a waste of money to try and aid people in poor countries of the Third World. What do you think?

If we could stockpile things for use in national disasters such as earthquakes or floods, what essential things would be needed?

Make lists. How could these stockpiles be organized for places like India, South America, Britain?

A charitable organization in England has a little money to help an eastern country devastated by war. Discuss the best way to use the money. Only *one* of the three ways is possible:

1 Send the cash to the foreign government's Health Department.
2 Build a large hospital in the worst area of devastation.
3 Send a small group of nurses and one doctor to give their services to the sick and wounded.

3.2 The Circus Clowns

Joey was a boy with a problem—he was always eating. He would eat his breakfast then ask for more cornflakes, then more toast and more cornflakes; and well before dinner time he was hungry again. He was always hungry; but the strange thing was that he was thin—the thinnest boy you ever saw.

'I don't know what you do with all that food,' said Joey's mother. 'You ought to be fat, not thin.'

Now Joey had a friend whose name was Gus, and Gus was fat. He was so fat that his mother put him on a special diet. But it made no great difference to his size—he was still fat. Gus's father used to say to him, 'Have a biscuit, Gus, while your mother is out. I'm sure you don't get enough to eat on that silly old diet.'

So Gus always had chocolate biscuits when his mother was out.

'I can't understand where that last packet of biscuits has gone,' Gus's mother would say; and Dad would pretend that *he* had eaten them.

You would never think that such different boys could be such good friends, but Gus and Joey really liked each other and never fell out about anything—well, hardly ever. They did argue sometimes—and always it was about which one was better at jumping or running or performing somersaults. They never argued for long.

One day, as they were going home arguing about who was better at balancing on the apparatus at school, Gus and Joey didn't see the huge trucks with brightly-painted signs; but a roar made them look.

'Joey,' said Gus. 'It's the circus.'

'Let's watch them on the field,' said Joey.

So they ran to the field where some of the circus tents were already erected. The biggest tent of all—the big top—was just being pulled into place by what seemed to be hundreds of men.

'The elephants are helping,' shouted Joey, quite excited because he liked elephants.

'I wonder where the lions are?' said Gus.

He was afraid of lions ever since one had roared quite close to him in the zoo.

'Let's go and help,' said Joey.

The two boys ran to a small tent which was being put up by three girls just a little older than the boys. The girls seemed glad of their help and soon the tent was pegged into place.

'Thank you boys,' said the biggest girl, who was dark haired and quite pretty. 'Would you like to see some of the circus acts?'

'Oh yes, please,' said Joey and Gus in the same breath.

'Especially the elephants,' said Joey.

'But not the lions,' said Gus.

'Come on then,' said the pretty girl whose name was Ann.

First they watched the zebras being unloaded and fed. Then the ponies were brought out and they galloped round the field; but one of the men gave a piercing whistle and all the ponies came round him and pushed him with their noses. They pushed so hard that the man fell over. Gus felt sorry for the poor man and wondered if the ponies would trample him.

'Don't worry about him,' said Ann. 'He's a clown and the ponies are trained to push him down over and over again. It's quite funny when he is dressed in clown's costume and he falls into a bath of water.'

Suddenly Gus jumped up and gave a little screech as something heavy fell right on his back.

'It's all right,' said Ann.

Joey just laughed. It was a baby chimp who had crept up to the boys and jumped on Gus. Now that Gus knew what it was, he felt quite pleased that the chimp had decided to jump on *him*.

It was the elephants' turn next to show off. Even Gus thought they were funny. The elephants had finished helping with the big tent and now they were playing together. They went round and round in a ring with each elephant holding the tail of the elephant in front. Then they suddenly stopped, right in front of the boys; and all together, they sat on their bottoms, raised their front legs right up in the air and swung their trunks up and just sat there.

Gus and Joey watched the seals playing with a ball, but the game was spoilt by the poodles who wanted to play too. The two boys never noticed the time so it was quite a shock when Ann called:

'Now you two, isn't it time you went home for tea?'

'I'd love to join the circus,' said Joey.

'And me,' said Gus.

'Not until you are older,' laughed Ann. 'Come back in five years' time.'

And they did.

It was just five years later when the circus came back. Joey and Gus had left school but hadn't found jobs.

'Let's join the circus,' said Joey to his friend.

They went to the field and the first person they met was Ann. She was a beautiful young lady but she remembered the boys—the one so fat and the other so thin.

'Hallo again,' she said. 'I never thought I should see you after all these years.'

'We want to work in the circus,' said Joey.

'Good,' said Ann. 'Just come with me and we'll find something for you to do.'

They wandered into the big tent where they watched the acrobats practising on the high trapeze.

'I want to do that,' said Gus.

'Sorry,' said the chief acrobat. 'You're a bit too heavy for this sort of work. But we'll give your friend a trial.'

So Joey started with the acrobats and Gus went to help with the animals. It was two days later that the lion-keeper felt ill so he asked Gus to feed the lions for him. Gus walked to the cage carrying the huge chunks of meat. He felt sick and trembly. Just as he got to the cage door, one huge lion roared and slashed between the bars with his paw. Gus dropped the meat and ran right into the big tent. He never saw Joey kneeling on the mat until it was too late to stop; and Gus dived right over Joey's back and made a perfect somersault. As he stood up he heard someone shout: 'That was marvellous. You're just the lad I'm looking for.'

Gus saw that it was the circus clown talking to him. So that is how Gus became a clown; and you can guess who joined him as another clown—Joey. They were clowns in the same circus for years and years, bringing happiness to thousands and thousands of children. And they were friends for ever.

Prayer/Thought

We don't need to be clowns in order to bring happiness to other people. A child's smile can often brighten the dismal thoughts of a grown-up; and a few kind words can work wonders.

Assembly ideas

Friendships in the Bible—Ruth and Naomi, David and Jonathan.
Great friendships—Helen Keller and Anne Sullivan, Damon and
    Phintias (Children's Britannica and Arthur Mee Encyclo-
    pedia), Scott and Bowers (*People in History* by R. J. Unstead,
    published by A. and C. Black 1967).

Activity and discussion ideas

How do you choose a friend?
How do you choose a friend of the opposite sex?
Can opposites make good friends? Do you know examples?
Can people of different colour be good friends?

3.3 A Boy and His Donkey

The town of Assisi in Italy is world famous. It is, of course, the home town of Saint Francis—the saint with so many legends about his understanding of birds and all animals. Assisi today is a busy market town with many visitors. The market place is filled with noisy animals from the Italian farms and amongst the people working there was a boy, Pepino, just ten years old. Pepino was poor, ragged and he never wore shoes because he couldn't afford to buy any. He had large ears and scrubby, short hair sticking up like a brush. But if you looked at him you would immediately notice his eyes—big and dark, with an appealing expression. Pepino was an orphan. His father, mother and all near relatives had been killed in the war. He looked after himself and his one friend. Pepino was an unusual orphan. He didn't think of himself as poor because he had inherited something—his friend. The friend was called Violetta—and she was a donkey.

Violetta was a good donkey—friendly and gentle with long pointed ears like any other donkey. But she was different. She had a strange expression around the corners of her mouth which made her appear to have a permanent smile. The combination of the smiling donkey and the boy's luminous dark eyes charmed most people into giving Pepino plenty of work, so that he was able to save a little money each week.

Pepino always treated Violetta gently and never hit her like the other donkey boys did their animals. She was more to him than a job: she was like a mother, father, brother and playmate. Every night they slept together in the stable. When he was happy, Pepino would sing softly into Violetta's gently moving ears; and when Pepino felt lonely and miserable, he would cry himself to sleep on her warm soft flanks. She loved him. To her, he was a god. Then one spring morning Pepino called out:

'Violetta, time to get up for the market.'

But Violetta just rolled over and went to sleep again.

'Violetta!' shouted Pepino. 'Hurry up. We shall miss the early trade.'

Violetta stood and the day went on as usual—or almost as usual; for Pepino had to shout at his donkey several times that day. She seemed to be tired and half asleep.

Next day, Violetta was even slower. Day after day she got slower and slower. Pepino noticed that she was looking thin; and most disturbing of all, Violetta had lost her smile. Pepino fetched some of his savings from his money-box and took Violetta to see Dr Bartoli, the vet, who examined her and said that she probably had a germ in her intestines.

'I am afraid your donkey is very sick,' Dr Bartoli said. 'Give her plenty of rest and light feeds.'

When Pepino got back to the stable, he put his head against Violetta's heaving flank and cried and cried. Then suddenly, he stopped crying as an idea occurred to him. He would call on the help of the good Saint Francis. He would take Violetta into the crypt of the church where Saint Francis had been buried 750 years before and he would pray for her to be healed. With great difficulty, Pepino got Violetta to rise; and now the feeble animal trotted through the narrow streets to the church entrance. There, Pepino asked Fra Bernard, the monk in charge, to let him take his friend into the crypt so that Saint Francis could cure her.

'You can't take that donkey into the crypt,' said Fra Bernard. 'Animals are not allowed into the church; and in any case, the stairs are hardly wide enough for two-legged humans; and certainly there is no room for a four-legged animal. Clear off.'

At first Pepino was miserable—but not for long. He remembered the advice of an old friend, an American soldier who was always saying, 'If you want to get on in this life, kid, never take no for an answer.'

So Pepino was more determined than ever. He would not give up. He went to see his good friend, the priest Father Damico, and asked for his advice.

'You are within your rights in taking your request to the supervisor of the church,' Father Damico advised. 'And if there is any difficulty in getting Violetta into the crypt, there is another entrance from below through the old church which has been walled up for over a hundred years.'

Pepino thanked his friend and hurried as fast as Violetta would allow to get to the supervisor's office. When he got there, the supervisor was talking to the Bishop. Pepino listened to the conversation and quickly realized that they were talking about Saint Francis.

'What a pity,' said the supervisor, 'that we have no relic of the good saint. If only we had a lock of his hair or a fingernail it would bring in many more tourists.'

When they noticed him standing near, Pepino was able to explain about his donkey—how she was very sick and the vet thought she might die; and that Saint Francis loved all animals, especially donkeys, and only the good saint could make her well; and he had to take her into the crypt where Saint Francis could really see her.

The supervisor was shocked by the very thought of an animal in the crypt.

'If I let such a thing happen,' he said, 'people will bring sick dogs, cats, goats or even pigs. The place will be like a pig sty!'

The Bishop was more sympathetic but he came up with the very practical problem of *how* the donkey could get into the crypt down the narrow stairway.

'I know another way,' said Pepino excitedly. 'There is another way from below, through the old church, which was walled up. Father Damico told me.'

'I am sorry,' said the Bishop, 'but the supervisor and I haven't the authority to allow anyone to make an entrance in the old church. It is not possible.'

This time Pepino felt defeated; but once more he thought of his American friend's advice—'Never take no for an answer'. So Pepino went to see Father Damico again. Father Damico tried to explain as simply as he could so that the boy could understand how the little town of Assisi was linked to Rome with Cardinals and other officials and the Vatican all in higher positions of authority; and over all was His Holiness the Pope. But they were all so busy with important things that Pepino and his donkey would never get a hearing. But Pepino had made up his mind. He went out and using his thumb in the way his American soldier friend had shown him, he hitched a lift in a lorry going to Rome. And so it was, early next morning, a ragged forlorn boy stood in the deserted square of St Peters. He felt lonely, frightened and unhappy. It was many minutes before Pepino had enough courage to walk across to one of the small entrances to the Vatican. The Swiss guard on duty looked enormous to little Pepino.

'Please,' said Pepino, 'I want to see the Pope. I want to speak to him about my donkey, Violetta.'

The guard, who had a boy at home about the same size as Pepino, just smiled. He said that the Pope was very busy and couldn't be seen; and as he spoke, he brought his great battle-axe down on the pavement near Pepino's toes just to show him he meant business. Dispirited, Pepino went away. But he thought of his American friend and was determined to try again. It was then that he noticed the old woman sitting under an umbrella selling little bunches of spring flowers. Pepino remembered how Father Damico had often said that Saint Francis had loved flowers. Perhaps the Pope liked flowers too. He bought a little bunch of mixed flowers with lilies of the valley on a bed of dark violets, a small red rose and a few yellow pansies all tied together with a leaf and feather fern and paper lace. Pepino then bought a post-card from the next stall and borrowed a pen to write out a message.

'Dear Holy Father. These flowers are for you. Please let me see you and tell you about my donkey Violetta who is dying and they will not let me take her to see Saint Francis so that he may cure her. I live in the town of Assisi and I have come all the way here to see you. Your loving Pepino.'

Then he returned to the entrance of the Vatican and gave the note and the bunch of flowers to the Swiss guard, asking him to take them to the Pope. The guard was very surprised. Those large trusting eyes of Pepino had a peculiar effect on him. He didn't want to upset the lad so he thought he would pretend to take the message but would spend a few minutes in the guard-room and then go and tell the boy that the Pope was grateful for the flowers but was too busy to grant him an audience. But when the guard got to the guardroom, he found, to his amazement, that he couldn't bring himself to throw the flowers in the waste bin. The flowers reminded him of his boyhood in a village in Lucerne and the Swiss mountains and the soft-eyed cattle grazing in the valleys. He wandered out into the corridor and bumped into a priest who was one of the secretaries employed in the Vatican. The secretary was surprised to see the big guard carrying the little bouquet and easily took them when the message was explained. He could throw them away; but he didn't, for he too was captured by the thought of spring flowers and he remembered with happiness the last time he had seen flowers like those in the little bunch he held. And so the bouquet was passed from hand to hand in that place so full of important people; and the magic and memory of happy days made it impossible for anyone to throw the flowers away. Eventually, they came to the great man himself. By now, the flowers had lost their freshness;

they had wilted, but the Pope looked and thought and read the note.

'Bring the boy to me,' he said.

So, perched on the edge of a chair, Pepino told his story about Violetta and her smile; his love for her and hers for him. He talked about her illness and how she could be taken into the crypt if permission could be given to open up the old entrance through the old church. Half an hour later, Pepino was sure he was the happiest boy in all the world. For after the Pope's blessing, he had been given two letters—one addressed to the supervisor of Saint Francis Monastery, Assisi and the other to Father Damico.

So it was, two days later, that Pepino and Violetta waited while the workmen broke through the old church entrance to the crypt and the Bishop, the supervisor and Father Damico watched and waited. When they broke through they found a small, grey, leaden box with 1226 and a large F on the side. It was opened and inside they found a piece of rope as used by the monks round their waist, a sprig of wheat, a dried-up stem of primrose and one tiny feather from a meadow bird. They stared, overcome at the relics left by the saint 750 years before. Pepino said: 'Please, may Violetta and I come into the crypt now?'

They all went in. Then Father Damico looked round and saw that the donkey was different. She was smiling.

Prayer/Thought
Pepino was a very persistent boy who would not take no for an answer when his friend was ill. We should be just as persistent in helping our human friends, even though it may not be easy.

Assembly ideas
Home—sharing difficulties, relations, neighbours, friends.
Special pets.
Partnership with an animal—shepherd and sheepdog, blind person and guide dog, man and hawk, girl and pony, trainer and dolphin.

Activity and discussion ideas
Explain what 'happiness' is and try to show how it differs from pleasure and jokes.

Write a few words about the happiest time you can remember and explain what caused the happiness.

3.4 Terry

Happiness is a contented family; and sometimes, everything seems to be against that family ever being happy. So it was with Terry and his family. The tiny baby was born in hospital in January 1962. The doctors told the mother that the little boy probably would not live—in fact, they said that she ought to think of him as dead. She did; and when she left the hospital, the mother left the baby behind. But he wasn't dead. The child was a Thalidomide baby—one of those babies born after the mother had taken medicine containing Thalidomide, which was later found to be a dangerous chemical, resulting in terribly deformed babies being born. That Thalidomide baby was later called Terry. He had no legs, no arms and no pelvic girdle; so he could never walk or even attempt to make any of the movements of a normal child. Terry had only one eye. He had two hand-like flippers sticking out of his trunk where arms would have been. Terry was put into a home for severely disabled children. His future was dismal.

Then Terry's luck changed; for two people adopted him. Leonard Wiles and his wife Hazel took Terry out of the home. They were the most unlikely people to be successful parents. Hazel had been married three times before. Leonard had a bad record at school and had never been able to keep a job for very long. They lived in a broken-down old cottage with very little furniture; in fact, they had very little of anything. When they took Terry out of the home, a new life started for Leonard and Hazel Wiles. They dedicated themselves to giving Terry freedom from a life governed by artificial limbs and the discipline of a special home for severely handicapped children. Leonard and Hazel were determined that Terry would be able to lead as normal a life as possible at home. Hazel spent hours and hours teaching and training Terry. Leonard helped in a different way; and his own experience in a wheelchair had convinced him that a special wheelchair would give Terry greater freedom. They spent all the time they could with Terry. Hazel once spent a whole afternoon just pushing Terry over so that he banged his head—until he learned to control the fall by breaking it with his shoulders. It was rough treatment done by a loving mother who was nearly in tears all the time she was doing it. She was trying to help Terry to fit into as normal an existence as possible. Leonard Wiles was a mechanical genius. He designed a special wheelchair like a super car which not only carried Terry around, but could also move up and down from table-top level to near to the floor; and best of all, it made it possible for Terry to go to a normal school.

Happiness came to three people—Leonard and Hazel Wiles and Terry; happiness they never thought possible.

'Terry made us a happy family of three,' said Leonard Wiles. 'And so say all of us,' said Terry and his mother.

Prayer/Thought

Leonard and Hazel were the most unlikely new parents for Terry; yet they succeeded in making a happy family because they had one thing to give in unlimited quantity—love.

Assembly ideas

Playlets depicting marriage, birth, childhood, leaving home, old age.

The problems of the family—bedtime, clothes, TV, pocket money, friends, neighbours.

Ask a teacher from a school for handicapped children to talk about his/her work.

Activity and discussion ideas

What organizations are there to help children like Terry?

Is it better for a handicapped child to be in a special school or would the child be happier in a normal school? What things would have to be done in an ordinary school to cater for someone like Terry?

Try writing with a pencil held in the teeth to get some idea of what a handicapped child may have to do.

3.5 A Pakistani Picnic

Shamuna liked her school in Yorkshire. She now understood English well enough to leave the special class; but she still felt embarrassed occasionally because the class had boys as well as girls. In Pakistan her last school was, of course, for girls only. Shamuna had an English friend called Susan in her new class.

It was summer and Susan telephoned Shamuna one day.

'Would you like to come with us for a picnic tomorrow about ten o'clock?'

'What is a picnic?' asked Shamuna.

Susan explained.

'Oh, I know,' said Shamuna. 'I will come.'

After she had replaced the receiver Shamuna thought of the picnic when she was at her last school in Pakistan. It was December; and in that part of Pakistan the weather was just right, with warm sunny days and cool nights.

'I know what we will do tomorrow,' said the Principal. 'We will have a picnic.'

Next day everyone was up early so that all could help with the preparations for the picnic. Everything had to be well planned because all the cooking would be done at the picnic site. There was great excitement when a bullock cart arrived to carry some of the bulky things. The girls eagerly loaded firewood, cooking pots, buckets, banana leaves, mats, a trenching spade and large curved vegetable knives. The bullock cart set off at a slow steady pace and some of the older girls left at the same time to walk to the picnic site. Then the Land Rover had to be loaded up with a big sack of rice, vegetables and two geese already plucked and cut into cooking pieces. Fifteen people managed to squeeze into the Land Rover and somehow they all managed the journey over the badly-rutted road without any bruises.

When the Land Rover arrived at the picnic site the bullock cart had been unloaded by the girls who had walked. It was a beautiful site, just outside a village and on the side of a lake. A trench had been dug by the bullock-cart driver and a fire was burning ready for the cooking. The pots were quickly filled with rice and water and then placed on the fire. In the meantime some of the girls were preparing the vegetables. Other girls took the buckets to the village and filled them with water from the tube well and then carried them back to the Land Rover. These first buckets of water were used to wash the banana leaves which would be used as plates. More water was fetched to wash hands because no knives, forks or spoons would be used. The rush mats were spread in a circle and each girl sat crosslegged whilst water was poured over her right hand. Then as one girl covered each banana-leaf plate with a small heap of rice, another girl followed with vegetables and everyone started eating. The next food to be delivered was lentil soup poured in a little hollow in another heap of rice on each leaf plate. After that came the main treat—delicious goose curry straight from the cooking pot. They only had meat on one day in most weeks so this was an extra treat. As soon as the diners had finished they changed places with the girls serving. When everyone had finished there was no washing up. The banana leaves were thrown away and the village dogs soon cleared up any food scraps. After that the girls played games until it was time to return to school.

'Will it be like that here in England?' thought Shamuna. 'No, perhaps not; but some things will be the same.'

Prayer/Thought
Children from other countries may find many things quite different from their last home; but there may be some things which are similar. If we can find such similarities it may make a happy link for a child in a strange country.

Assembly ideas
Short play about family spreading litter after English picnic, in a field. The farmer arrives and makes them take the litter away.
A picnic is the sharing of food. Compare with the Bible story of Jesus and the loaves and fishes.
Sharing and friendship. Children give short talk about their special friend with large picture.

Activity and discussion ideas
How does the Pakistani picnic differ from an ordinary English picnic? Which would be more fun?

Why is a picnic usually more enjoyable than an ordinary meal in a house?

Think about the machines used during a normal day in Britain for a boy or girl. Compare with a child in rural Pakistan.

3.6 Diwali in England

The three boys just stood there shouting: 'Go on Paki!'

At least, it sounded like that. Khamla was with his friend Ragu, walking home from school.

'What did they say?' asked Khamla.

'They are shouting "Go home Paki!" That is what they mean by "Go on Paki".'

'Paki! Paki! I'm not from Pakistan. They are stupid.'

'They think we are all from Pakistan. They are ignorant savages.'

Khamla wondered why the ignorant boys shouted at him. Then he saw them running and he heard the tinkle of falling glass as a stone hit a window. Those three boys were hooligans—unfriendly and spiteful. His friend would never do anything like that.

Khamla's thoughts wandered. He remembered coming to England from Kenya; and he still had some memories of India. His parents often told him stories about the village where his grandparents lived. They reminded him about the exciting festivals—especially Diwali, the Festival of Lights. Everyone was on holiday for at least two days to enjoy the fun. Khamla's family sent Diwali cards to their relatives and friends. All the people who could afford it bought new clothes; and his mother had a beautiful new sari and she wore all her golden bangles.

When his family moved to England, Khamla found that things were very different. When October came, he thought about the Diwali holiday; but on the day of Diwali his father went to work and Khamla went to school; and no one even mentioned Diwali. No one sent any cards at school. There were no parties.

Khamla wondered why the other boys at school who looked as if they came from India did not remember it was Diwali. He was so excited that he found himself talking in Gujerati to one group of boys. They didn't appear to understand him; and then he found that no one came from South India. One boy was from North India, three from Pakistan and two from Bangladesh. They all spoke their own language like Urdu or Hindi. Later, Khamla tried out his African language on some black-skinned boys from another class. He found out that they had never been in Africa and they actually came from the West Indies. Khamla decided that they could talk together in only one language— English. One of the teachers was interested in the group. Together they looked at a globe and they found the different countries where their parents were born; but most of the children had been born in England. The teacher explained that the children all had special festivals but they were sometimes at different times of the year. She said that they would try to fit them all in at school; so Khamla felt much happier with the prospect of Diwali lights for the next year and perhaps cards too. In any case, he had many friends now. He even managed to teach them a few words in Gujerati.

Prayer/Thought

Some people are hostile to anyone who looks different—perhaps with a different-coloured skin. It is not easy to understand other children who may speak another language. We are all human and can all be good neighbours, living in peace and friendship.

Assembly ideas

Dramatized version of the classical Hindu story of Rama and Sita.

Small groups present scenes illustrating Diwali, Yom Kippur, Hanukkah, Ramadhan, Baqr Eid.

Scenes from West Indies, Africa, Pakistan, India, Bangladesh.

Wedding customs in different countries.

Activity and discussion ideas

Can you think of ten different things to discuss about India? For example, great leaders, climate, religions etc.

Are there any festivals like Diwali in other religions?
What do we mean by 'neighbourliness'?
Read the words of 'When I needed a neighbour' by Sidney
   Carter, *Songs for the Seventies*, Galliard.

4 COURAGE

4.1 Rescuing the Rescuer

For the first time for over a week it was a fine day; and the sun made it feel warm although it was just the beginning of March. Bridgette and Katie decided to walk across the meadows and look at the flooded fields.

'Look at that water over there,' Katie called to her older sister. 'We could paddle in it.'

'All right,' said Bridgette.

The two girls took off shoes and socks and paddled in the over-flowing floodwater on the banks of the brook.

'Can you feel the water pulling on your legs?' shouted Bridgette to her sister, who was some distance away.

There was no reply from Katie and Bridgette looked behind to see why she didn't answer. She was just in time to see Katie swept along the bank and into the main stream of the brook. Quickly Bridgette splashed her way to Katie and began to swim when it was too deep for running. The floodwater was pulling strongly like a tide and Bridgette had great difficulty in swimming to her sister. At last she was near enough to grab Katie and turn her on her back. Katie couldn't swim and she was only seven. The two girls were swept away by the current into the brook and downstream. Try as she could, Bridgette could not make any headway against the strong pull of the current. She felt herself tiring and she began to feel the deadly chill of the cold water. Something brushed against her face and, without thinking, she grabbed hold. It was the branch of a tree which had been up-rooted and jammed in the brook. The branch was strong and the two girls held on.

Meanwhile, on the bank, two men raced along and one plunged into the water. It was the girls' father. He entered the water downstream; and so he had to swim up against the current. He had a line tied to his waist and this was held by some men who had just arrived. At last the father reached his daughters but he was now exhausted and his feeble attempt to pull them to safety failed. He held on to Katie but Bridgette was swept away.

Now the second man was in the water and he swam strongly to the father and child. It was Police Constable Cooper. He was fully dressed and his uniform dragged as it got wet. The twenty metres to the branch seemed more like a kilometre. He got there and pulled the exhausted father and Katie to safety.

But what had happened to Bridgette? Fortunately she had floated further downstream and had grabbed at the branch of another tree. She was now slightly nearer to the Police Constable. He plunged in again and battled through the water to Bridgette. But now he was very tired and he never reached her. He was pulled back by the men holding the line. He tried again and again. He never remembered how many attempts he made to reach Bridgette. His mind was as numb as his body was cold. But he forced himself to have a last try. He kept telling himself to keep going, to keep on and on and on. He never heard the cheer of the crowd but he felt the sharp sting of a branch on his face; and then he had the girl. They were hauled back to safety with the rope.

All four, wet and shivering, were taken into a car and they were just about to start when P.C. Cooper snapped out of his daze.

'Wait a bit,' he said, 'where's my helmet?'

And they had to go and look for it before going on to hospital for a check-up.

Prayer/Thought
We think of policemen and policewomen; and we wish them all help in their difficult work.

Assembly ideas
Use plays from the first activity idea below.
Safety as a general theme.

Activity and discussion ideas
Firemen, police, lifeguards, lifeboatmen, helicopter crews often have to rescue people who have acted foolishly. Think out

examples and make up plays to illustrate your ideas on how people can behave sensibly in dangerous places.

Find out what percentage of children in your class can swim; and then how many are capable of rescuing another child who is a non-swimmer and out of her depth.

Make up a notice or a drawing to keep young children from dangerous water.

Make up a set of rules on safety for young children who go to the seaside on holiday.

4.1 A Loyal Answer to a Searching Question

Spy films on television often show someone brought in for questioning by an interrogator. It may be the SS officer trying to break the escape network and getting the names of people in the resistance group. If the person being questioned gives no information away he is showing courageous loyalty to his friends and to his country. He is being true and faithful, which is what loyalty means.

Sometimes you may have to show loyalty to your family even though you may not agree with the grown-ups about something. But in some countries children are encouraged to tell about their mothers and fathers: to give information about them so that they are sent to prison. In those countries there is no loyalty to the family—only to the government.

In times of war, most people are loyal to their country and they will do anything to help their country to win the war. But what if the war is a civil war: that is a war within the country, with Englishmen fighting against Englishmen? There was a civil war in England three centuries ago when Cromwell's men (Roundheads) fought against the King's army (Cavaliers); and every family supported either the King or Cromwell. Even the children sometimes had their loyalty and courage tested. One story is famous because of a picture painted by an artist called William Frederick Yeames. His painting shows a young boy

57

standing in front of a table facing a Roundhead officer who is questioning him. The title of the picture is a question—'When did you last see your father?'

The boy's father was a Cavalier officer in the King's army which had just suffered defeat. King Charles had disappeared and Cromwell's men were searching every place where the King might be hiding. The troop of Cromwell's soldiers came to the boy's home because his father was known to be a captain in the King's army. They searched the house and grounds but had no luck. Then the Roundhead officer questioned the captain's family. The boy was present when his mother and one of his sisters was interrogated by the officer, and he knew that they were desperately trying to conceal their knowledge of the captain's hiding place; and they would do anything to protect his father. The young boy guessed that his turn would come for interrogation, and then what would he say? He had been brought up to believe that to tell a lie was a terrible sin, but how could he answer and not give away his father? He was startled out of his thoughts when he heard one of the Roundhead officers call him to the table for questioning. The boy went slowly up to the table and stood upright and still, looking at the stern face of the interrogating officer. One of the soldiers looked at him and said, 'Now, think carefully and tell us the truth.'

Then another of the Roundhead officers said, 'When did you last see your father?'

The boy felt the words burn in his brain. He felt hot, then cold with fear, but he stood upright and faced the enemy officers with no fear showing in his face. At that moment his mother looked at her young son and thought how like his father he was. As she looked at him the boy replied, 'I looked at my father yesterday, and I remembered well his last words to me. He told me to serve my King and country: to be loyal.'

'Yes. Yes. Go on,' said the interrogator.

'My father has told me that one day the fighting would be over and everyone would have to help rebuild our country: to make it better than it ever was before.'

'Yes. Yes!' said the interrogator. 'Where did you see your father? Take us to him.'

'Come this way,' said the boy.

The chief interrogator and a party of Roundhead soldiers went with the boy through the main hall and through several passages until they reached a small room. There they slowed and walked stealthily to the door at the end. The boy stopped and opened the door. In the small room was a bed and a table.

'Whose room is this?' asked the Roundhead officer.

'It is my room,' said the boy.

'Where is your father?' asked the officer.

The boy pointed to the wall facing the bed and said, 'I looked at my father in that picture every night before I slept. I always remembered his last words to me.'

'When did he speak to you?' asked the officer.

'It was six months ago,' said the boy, 'before my father went away to fight. That was the last time my father spoke to me.'

'You have wasted my time,' cried the Roundhead officer. 'Get out of my sight.'

The boy went out of the room knowing he had not told a lie, and sure that his father's hiding place would be safe.

Prayer/Thought

We may find it difficult to decide what to do or say if our loyalty is tested. We should be guided by our conscience so that the action we take is for good; and we should never be tempted to help evil people or to do evil things.

Assembly ideas

Groups of children combine in a Festival of Courage with each
    group portraying one courageous individual or act including
    the boy in the picture 'When did you last see your father?'

Courage of the pioneers—the first to do something really cour-
    ageous: sailing the Atlantic single-handed, climbing Mt
    Everest, reaching the Poles, swimming the Channel.

Activity and discussion ideas

What would you do if your loyalty was tested at school by a
    teacher you liked who was questioning you about a friend who
    had broken the school rules?

If you were really brave enough, what would you like to do?

Find examples of courageous acts in reading books and newspapers and discuss why you think they show courage.

4.3 Don Quixote

If you have ever had a holiday in Spain, you will have seen, in the
shops, lots of things carved in wood. Often the carvings are of
people; and one of the most popular is of a tall, thin man with a
lance carved in wood from the olive tree. The carving is of a man
we call Don Quixote.

Don Quixote was a man in a story written nearly 400 years
ago. Don Quixote read so many books about knights in shining
armour that he thought of nothing else. One day, he was looking
round the cellar under his house when he noticed a heap of rusty
metal in one dark corner. He kicked it hard and then yelled out
because it hurt his foot. He looked closer and found that the rusty
metal was really old armour, and with it was a big sword.

'I can be a knight,' he said to himself.

He spent all the next ten days cleaning the armour and trying
it on for size. It fitted him like a suit of clothes; but there was one
bit missing from the part of the helmet which would protect his
face, so he made a face-piece out of thick paper and fitted it to the
helmet.

'That will do quite well,' he said to himself. He often talked
aloud to himself.

'I must have a good, strong horse,' he said.

He went to the stable and looked at his horse. It was really a
poor old thin mule and not like the sort of horse a knight should
ride; but Don Quixote thought his horse looked strong and good
for many a battle.

Next day, Don Quixote rode on his horse, intending to go to a
castle where the Lord could make him a knight. He rode all day
and all night until he came to a village inn. The landlord came
running when he saw Don Quixote, all in armour, on his horse.

'Good evening, sir,' said Don Quixote. 'I have come for you
to make me a knight.'

The landlord pretended to follow Don Quixote's wishes and touched Don Quixote's shoulder with the big sword and said: 'I name you Knight. Rise, Sir Knight.'

So, from then on, Don Quixote thought he was a real knight and he rode away quite pleased with himself. At least he was pleased with everything except one little problem—he couldn't get the helmet off his head so he had to keep it on all day and sleep in it at night. It was very heavy so he was feeling a bit tired. As he rode on, Don Quixote thought it would be rather nice to have a companion; and he decided to ask Sancho Panza to come with him as his squire. Sancho Panza was a fat man with short legs. He came along on his donkey because he had no money to buy a horse. They rode on across the flat land when suddenly Don Quixote called out:

'Look at those giants!'

'I can't see any giants,' said Sancho.

'Over there, can't you see?' said Don Quixote.

'I can only see some windmills,' said Sancho.

But he was talking to himself because Don Quixote was galloping towards the windmills at full speed—or at least as fast as his poor old horse would move. Don Quixote attacked the first windmill with his lance which stuck in a sail; but just at that moment, the wind blew and Don Quixote, holding onto the lance, was pulled right off his horse and up high in the air. He let go of the lance and dropped in a heap on the ground.

'Help me, Sancho,' shouted Don Quixote, because he couldn't get up when he was weighed down with his suit of heavy armour. Sancho helped him and they rode on, again looking for adventure.

Sancho was thinking that Don Quixote was very silly; but he knew that his knight had a kind heart and would always try to help people. As he was thinking these thoughts, Sancho suddenly saw a line of men staggering towards them with their necks all chained together and each with handcuffs on their wrists. With them were four guards all with guns and swords.

'What's this?' asked Don Quixote.

'They are prisoners being taken to the King's ships. They are slaves.'

Don Quixote rode over to the guards and asked them why the men were chained and being taken to ships. They told him that some had stolen food and one was a cattle thief. But some had done nothing wrong at all.

'This is unfair,' shouted Don Quixote. 'No man should be a slave. These kind guards will let you all go free.'

When the guards heard this, they all fell about laughing; but soon stopped when Don Quixote charged them. The prisoners joined in the fight and the four guards ran away. The prisoners broke off the chains and handcuffs and escaped.

So, for once, Don Quixote thought that he had done something really worthwhile; and Sancho Panza thought so too.

Prayer/Thought

Don Quixote was a silly man but he had a kind heart and his silliness was really because he had high ideals based on what he thought a good knight should do. He never lacked courage; and eventually his brave action was responsible for freeing the slaves. We need idealists with courage more than ever today.

Assembly ideas

People in uniform—especially service to the community.

'The one thing I would like to change.' (Invite people to talk about something they would like to change and what they would do.)

Activity and discussion ideas

What changes would you like to see in schools?

Display hats and badges of organizations to which children belong. Link with people in uniform engaged in some form of community service.

What other people also help the community but have no distinguishing uniform?

4.4 Nansen and the Fram

Most children like to go on a sledge in the snow; and one of the best kinds of sledge used today was designed many years ago by a man called Nansen. Nansen was a scientist and explorer—an unusual combination for those days at the end of the nineteenth century. He was also a champion skier. He was fascinated by stories of the Arctic and he made several long journeys across ice and snow. He particularly wanted to be the first man to get to the North Pole; and he had a rather strange idea of how he could get there. It was an idea which depended on the special shape of a new ship called the *Fram*. 'Fram' is a Norwegian word meaning forward. When people saw the *Fram* being built they said it would never go anywhere; in fact, everybody laughed at the *Fram*. It was such a funny shape, with its length three times the width. It looked like a great fat slug before the three masts and small engine were fitted. There had never been a ship like her; but Nansen had been laughed at before and he didn't mind. He had the idea of making a ship strong enough to stay with the ice pack in the Arctic. He thought that the ship would be squeezed by the closing ice as it froze and then (if his theory was right) the ship would be pushed up and would lie on the ice. Previous explorers all had tall thin ships to sail through the pack-ice and many had been crushed. Nansen had another theory that the ice itself drifted from the Siberian Arctic Sea to the east coast of Greenland—so crossing the North Pole; and he thought his ship could drift with the ice.

Nansen and his men in the *Fram* crossed the rough Barents Sea which lies to the north of Russia, and sailed on through the ice-floes and dangerous fog. By September they had been at sea for three months and supplies of food were dangerously low; so they went on a walrus hunt. Nansen and two of the crew brought a small boat near a herd of walrus lying on a small ice-floe. Nansen fired two shots and killed two walrus. As they went to pick them up, the rest of the herd dived into the sea and attacked the boat. The men just managed to pull the dead walrus aboard and then they pulled away. It was a near thing.

By October the ice was really thickening; and soon it would be the dark Arctic winter. By the New Year, the ice was building up into huge ridges and one ice ridge was towering right over the *Fram*. The crew prepared sleges with equipment ready-packed to abandon the ship if the *Fram* was crushed. Suddenly the mass of ice and snow broke away and crashed onto the deck. One of the crew, Sverdrup, was taking a bath at the time and he rushed up on deck and was nearly crushed by the ice beating down. He had no clothes on so he went below to get dressed; and by the time he got back on deck, he decided that the *Fram* would be all right. The ship stood up to the ice and rolled free, then settled safely into the ice cradle. The strange shape of the *Fram* had been just right.

The *Fram* drifted with the ice just as Nansen had predicted; but the ship didn't get to the North Pole. Nansen decided to go with one other man, Johansen, with a sledge to the Pole. They started on March 14th, 1895 and they struggled on to within 360 kilometres of the North Pole. Then they had to turn back. No other man had ever gone as near as that. It was June 1896, more than a year later, when they met Jackson, an Englishman, leading another expedition. So they returned to Norway in another ship called the *Windward*. Shortly afterwards, the *Fram* was reported safe and all the crew well.

Nansen was never able to go on another expedition like that and he lent the *Fram* to another Norwegian, Amundsen, who became the first man to reach the *South* Pole.

Later on, Nansen spent all his time working to bring home millions of prisoners after World War 1. Then he worked for refugees and he was given the Nobel Peace Prize. So the man who had risked his own life so many times was able to save the lives of hundreds of thousands of people.

Prayer/Thought
Like most brave men, Nansen was always concerned about the safety of others. The courage which had served him so well in the Arctic was needed, later, when he had to overcome so many obstacles in repatriating prisoners of war and refugees.

Assembly ideas
Great achievements in medicine: Harvey, Lister, Pasteur, Ross, Fleming.
Climbing Everest: Hillary and Tenzing.
In space: Armstrong, Borman, Lovell, Anders.
Travel on land, sea, air.

Activity and discussion ideas

Plan essentials to take on a world voyage by a family in a small
   boat.

What things are a challenge to young people today?

Are children more adventurous today than they were in your
   parents' day?

5 SAFETY AND DANGER

5.1 The Bonfire

The three boys met as usual on Saturday afternoon. It was just a year since they had moved into the new houses and formed their gang. Colin was the leader because he was older (though only by a few months); but it was Richard who had the ideas. Matt just joined in everything because he couldn't stand quarrelling. The three friends played football for an hour on the bit of field still not built-up with houses. The game ended suddenly when Matt kicked the ball over the fence of the motorway. All three boys stood on top of the fence and looked over the steep, grassy slope but there was no sign of the ball. Twenty metres below, the lines of cars showed no break in the traffic from the tunnel of the bridge connecting the top road to their estate. They had seen it all so many times and the crowded M62 no longer interested them.

'Tell you what,' said Richard, 'let's go to the shed.'

'Good idea,' said Colin. 'Come on.' And he jumped down and ran ahead to the builders' hut which they called the old shed. It was no longer used by the builders who were now building houses on another site.

'Do you think they will ever come back to this shed?' asked Matt when they were all inside.

'No,' said Richard. 'I think they've forgotten it.'

'Well, it's ours now,' said Colin.

For five minutes the boys sat on boxes and chatted. Then Matt went over to one corner and picked up something.

'Look at this,' said Matt.

'Looks like the glass from an old torch,' said Colin. 'My dad used to have one like that.'

'It's the sort to use as a burning glass,' said Richard. 'Let's try it.'

The three boys rushed outside and Matt tried the burning glass on his hand, keeping the small spot of light quite still on one place.

'Ouch. It works all right,' said Matt. 'What can we do with it?'

'Oh, let's find that ball,' said Colin, who had lost interest in the burning glass.

The three boys climbed the motorway fence and started looking for the ball.

'I've found it,' said Matt.

'I've got an idea,' said Richard. 'Let's try that burning glass on this rubbish and see if we can burn it.'

Matt focused the glass over the dried twigs and grasses. In three minutes the little heap was smoking; and a minute later a tiny flame moved slowly from twig to stick and the bonfire had started.

'Fetch some more dry stuff,' shouted Colin.

At first it was just a small bonfire; but then the wind changed and the fire spread rapidly to the dried grass left by the mowing machine and Colin could see that it was getting out of hand. The three boys did their best to stamp out the grass fires but they were now too numerous for them to control.

On the motorway Mr Swift was thinking he would soon be at Hornsea and his two little children would be able to spend all next day on the sands. Then he saw the smoke. He braked sharply and then changed his mind and he accelerated to get through the blinding, choking smoke as quickly as possible. He never saw the car ahead which had braked hard and was now crawling at a very low speed through the smoke which was worse than thick fog. The Swifts' car hit the car in front and Mr Swift lost consciousness immediately. Before Mrs Swift could do anything, another car crashed into the back. Then another car and another crashed into the wreckage. There were nine cars in the pile-up. There was silence for a whole minute—then the children began to scream.

When the police came to see Colin, Richard and Matt next day, the boys admitted starting the bonfire. The policeman showed them the newspaper with the headline, 'M62 pile-up injures 14'.

'I didn't think it would cause trouble on the motorway,' said Colin.

'Your thoughtlessness could have caused the death of all those people,' said the policeman. 'There were children in three of the cars—and one was a baby of six months.'

Prayer/Thought

Let us think how something that seems to be harmless fun can have tragic consequences. Road safety is not just behaving correctly. It is also thinking of others and doing nothing to harm them. Children who drop things on motorways, or throw stones or even light bonfires near main roads may injure innocent people and could be killers.

Assembly ideas

Display of posters by children to illustrate safety: pills and medicines secure and labelled; fires and bonfires, spin dryers and overheating etc. Children explain about each poster and its purpose.

Talks/films by police on road safety.

Activity and discussion ideas

What would you do if you were in a situation (like Colin, Richard and Matt) where a fire was out of control?

List all the things in the home which could be dangerous, stating why. Make up small plays to illustrate each dangerous situation and a sensible, safe solution.

Each child takes one kind of danger inside buildings and writes about it. Outside dangers may be studied in the same way.

5.2 Sea Rescue in Hell's Mouth

It was August and holiday carnival time in St Ives, Cornwall. Mike Peters heard the heavy thud of a rocket which, to the holiday-makers outside, would appear to be the start of a firework display; but Mike knew what it was; and he leaned out of the window to see the maroon break. From the wardrobe he grabbed an old pair of trousers and a warm, blue jersey with the letters RNLI on it. Minutes later he was racing to the harbour. When he got there, the lifeboat was already out of the shed and slipping down the runway pulled by a tractor. Quickly Mike jumped aboard. He was the crew mechanic so his first job was to check the engine controls. As he did his checks, the other crew-men came aboard—Coxswain Dan Roach and his son Martin, Signalman Dan Paynter, Bowman Tom Cocking, Assistant Mechanic Jack Paynter and Crewman Richard Lander. Seven men—a full turn out.

'What is it?' Mike asked Coxswain Dan Roach.

'It's Hell's Mouth,' said Dan Roach. 'There are four people trapped in the cave.'

There had been five people in the cave but Harry Davis had made an escape bid. The first attempt to escape had been tried by a young Swede called Hans Bergessen who had climbed the rope they had used to drop into the cave shaft. But the rope was slippery with water and Hans had lost his grip at six metres and fallen. His head had struck the rocks and he was knocked un-conscious. When the others reached him they saw that he had a nasty head wound. Whilst the two Davis children Nina and Rus-sell and their Swiss girlfriend looked after Hans, Mr Davis decided to try and swim out of the tunnel before the tide turned. He had an easy start with the thirty-metre swim to the cave entrance and then he trod water and looked for a place to land and climb Hell's Mouth. The jagged rocks looked menacing but he knew that there was no alternative. He swam to a projecting ledge and hauled himself out of the water. Then he began his slow exhausting climb. His sodden clothing hung heavily and he quickly realized that he was in no condition for cliff climbing. He struggled on, breathing heavily and stopping every few metres to conserve his strength. Then it happened. He reached for a hold on a smooth projecting rock, his hand slipped and he felt himself falling eight metres down. He hit the sea with a force that knocked all the breath from his lungs. He surfaced and trod water, desperately snatching breath and looking for a place to land. Again he tried the ledge and began his slow painful ascent. It was 300 metres to the top; and it just had to be done. He crawled and hauled up the nearly sheer face of the rocks. He climbed and climbed until the blood rushing in his head made him doubt if he would ever see the top. Then he was there; one last haul and then over onto the grass. He couldn't move for several minutes until the spasm of exhaustion had passed; and then he walked drunken-ly, staggering to the road. A car stopped and took Harry Davis to a café where he dialled 999. Then he returned to the cliff top to watch for the lifeboat.

The St Ives' lifeboat went close in to Hell's Mouth—too close according to some of the watchers who remembered the last time a St Ives' lifeboat had been to Hell's Mouth. That time, the boat had smashed on the rocks and only one survivor had got ashore. Coxswain Dan Roach remembered too as he steered his boat as close as he dared.

'Better cast off the skiff now,' he said to Dan Paynter.

It had been a last minute inspiration to bring Dan's rowing boat to row into the cave entrance. Now the skiff was manned by Dan Paynter, Jack Paynter, Martin Roach and Tom Cocking and they pulled away into the cave entrance. They took the boat well into the tunnel entrance, then the swell caught her and lifted the boat right up and then she dropped with a sickening crash onto a jagged rock. The four lifeboatmen managed to struggle to the ledge where the frightened teenagers pulled them up. There they found the injured Hans Bergessen who was still semi-consciousness. The smashed skiff sank. The incoming tide was rising quickly and the lifeboatmen reckoned that in less than an hour the tunnel to the sea would be completely filled with water. They tried to persuade the youngsters to swim with them to the entrance; but the children were afraid and poor Hans refused to move.

'Me not go in water. Me not go in water,' he said over and over again.

'Wait here. I'll go back,' shouted Dan Paynter as he plunged into the water. He waded into the tide water and thrust on to the entrance where the water now reached the roof. Dan took a deep breath and pushed forward, clawing his way through and up. He surfaced and spluttered and thrashed the water. He was a non-swimmer; and although he wore a life jacket, he was tossed by the swell and waves broke over his head so that he nearly lost consciousness. He never saw the lifebelt thrown towards him; and it was Mike Peters who realized who it was and plunged from the deck of the lifeboat and pulled the exhausted signalman aboard. Minutes later, Dan Paynter had recovered and offered to struggle back to the cave with a rope.

'Oh no you don't,' said Coxswain Roach. 'Mike will go.'

Mike Peters went into the water with a light line tied to his middle and carrying spare life jackets. He swam with the tide into the cave, past the broken planks of the skiff, and to the ledge now waist-deep in water. Later on when talking about his rescue swim he said that the most terrible part of it was the thunderous noise of the sea breaking in the cave. He heard it in nightmares for years afterwards.

Now with Mike Peters on the ledge, the light line was hauled in and a heavier rope pulled in together with a breeches buoy for the injured Swede. Mike Peters fastened the rope to each of the seven in turn, then lashed Hans securely in the breeches buoy.

'I'm going back to the cave mouth. Hang on until you feel the rope pulling; then push out as fast as you can,' said Mike.

Mike Peters swam towards the entrance—sometimes under water as the sea touched the tunnel roof. At last he came out into the daylight. He found the rope, then he backed up to a rock and pushed the rope down with his stockinged feet to tighten it and clear the sharp rocks near the cave entrance. He felt the rope move under his feet and knew that they were hauling from the lifeboat. He pushed down harder to tighten the rope and held on to the rock.

'How long?' he thought.

Then a head and shoulders bobbed out of the cave entrance. Then another and another until all seven were clear and hauled aboard the lifeboat. Soon all the cave victims were ashore and in an ambulance. The weary lifeboatmen split up as each man walked to his home. Mike Peters squelched into his house and a few minutes later he was soaking blissfully in a hot bath. He could hear the sounds of the carnival. The tourists were enjoying themselves in St Ives. Gradually the sound grew fainter and fainter and Mike began to snore.

It was the end of another day in the lifeboatman's diary.

Prayer/Thought

Lifeboatmen and coastguards are often called out because of foolish behaviour by people on holiday. We should all take care —not only for our own safety, but also to ensure that rescue teams are not put at risk in trying to rescue us.

Assembly ideas

Improvise a play to show how each member of a team plays a
  vital part in helping to provide the strength of unity: the
  RNLI; the Coastguard Service; Air–Sea Rescue.

Activity and discussion ideas

Holidays—discussion on all the risks and dangers when on a
  holiday by the sea.

Holidays at home, on water (sea and canal), camping and cara-
  vanning. What are the dangers?

5.3 The Hole in the Ground

Richard and Helen were soon to go on holiday with their
mother, father and their friends Mark and Sandra. For the very
first time they were having a holiday away from the seaside.
They were staying in a caravan. When Helen's mum had first
asked the children if they would like a different holiday near
mountains and streams, Richard, who was listening for once
said:

'Can we sleep in a tent?'

'Well,' said Richard's mother, 'I don't know about that. We
were thinking of using Mr Stone's caravan.' (Mr Stone was
Mark and Sandra's father.)

'Oh, let's take our tent. We don't want a silly old caravan,'
said Richard.

'If you're going to talk like that,' said his mother, 'we shan't
be going with Mark and Sandra.'

Richard was quiet then while he thought that over.

'Could we take our tent just to sleep in?' said Helen. 'There
won't be much room if we all have to sleep in the caravan.'

'That's true,' said her mother. 'Eight of us in that caravan
would be hopeless. I'll talk to Daddy about it.'

'Oh good,' shouted Richard. 'I'm going to see Mark now and
tell him.'

And Richard was out of the house and next door before his

mother could say anything. Mark was just coming out of his house so Richard quickly explained about the caravan/tent holiday. Then they both rushed in to tell Mrs Stone. Poor Mrs Stone didn't know what to say when the children tried to explain, with both speaking at once; but fortunately, Richard's mum came in and the two mothers talked it over and agreed that it would be a good idea to take a tent for the children.

One week later it was the great day—the start of the holiday; and everyone was excited. Richard was in trouble before they started because he irritated his mother so much when she was trying to pack. The two families went in their own cars; but Mr Stone's car, of course, had to pull the caravan; so Richard's dad had to drive slower than usual. Richard kept saying, 'Go faster, Dad' so many times that even Helen had to tell him to shut up.

At last they reached their site. There were no other caravans or tents nearby and only one house could be seen. The children soon found that the house was empty and it was locked up. There were notices all round the door. Helen read one and said that the house belonged to a caving club in Yorkshire.

'Let's explore,' said Richard and he ran, followed by Mark, up the hill into the rough bracken.

The two girls followed, but the boys had gone out of sight. Richard and Mark ran on and on until they were tired. Just as they were climbing a rough line of large stones, Richard said:

'Look at this hole.'

The two boys peered down the hole in the ground. They could see that it was quite deep; and as they listened, they could hear running water.

'It's an underground river,' said Mark.

'Let's look for a bigger hole,' said Richard and he ran on.

In less than a minute they found something quite curious. It was a big circular piece of metal in the ground. It had a strange padlock. Richard pulled at the lock and it opened. Then he tugged at the large metal disc.

'It's moving,' said Mark as the metal disc slid sideways and the two boys looked down into a deep shaft.

'We can climb down this,' said Richard as he noticed a rough ladder on the side of the shaft.

Richard was first into the hole and slowly he felt his way down the ladder, followed by Mark. As they went lower and lower, it grew darker and darker; and they could hear running water.

'It's the underground river,' said Mark.

Mark's voice sounded strange. Suddenly there was a crash as Richard fell to the bottom, and another crash as Mark fell on top of him. They were not hurt, but Mark had rolled into some very cold water and he was not feeling very happy about it.

'Let's go back,' said Mark.

But when they felt around in the dark, they couldn't find the ladder at all. They groped around for several minutes before it dawned on them that they had fallen the last two metres because the ladder didn't go right down to the bottom. Then Richard tried to climb up but the sides were too smooth and slippery with water. Mark tried but he slipped and fell into water for the second time. Tears began to roll down his cheeks.

'They'll find us,' said Richard, who was a bit sorry for his friend.

It seemed hours and hours later when the boys saw a light hovering above them and a familiar voice called out:

'Richard. Mark. Are you there?'

It was Richard's dad and Mark's father right behind him. One by one the boys were hauled up with the aid of a strong rope. Then they were taken back to the caravan; and that first night the two boys slept in the caravan—without a murmur from either of them. It wasn't until next day that they had a family conference when the two boys agreed that it was not safe to go off without warning; and it was dangerous to go down a hole on your own.

Prayer/Thought

Our interest in adventure may often lead us into trouble. Our parents may be worried and so may be quite angry with us for getting into danger. We should remember that our parents' love for us may cause them to take somewhat drastic action when we take unnecessary risks.

Assembly ideas

Work of the mountain rescue, cave rescue and mining rescue teams.

Fire Brigade rescue service.
St John's Ambulance Brigade and Red Cross.

Activity and discussion ideas
Make up a set of rules for a pot-holing club so that all new
    members know the rules for safe pot-holing.
What outdoor activities do you consider are dangerous? Do you
    think there should be an age-level restriction on these ac-
    tivities?

5.4 A Corrugated Accident

Mr John Spencer was the owner of the Spencer Ironworks in
Birmingham. He was quite a rich man because his factory was
making iron rails for the railways spreading across England just
over a hundred years ago. The iron works were hot and noisy
and Richard, the new lad, was excited at his first day at work
after leaving school. He watched the huge machines crushing
hot metal into different shapes and the heavy hammers made the
floor quiver with vibrations. One machine was making railway
lines by crunching steel into a long continuous shape like an
upside-down U. Then, as Richard watched, something happened so quickly that he was not able to shout a warning even if
he had thought to do so. There were four men working on the
rail-making machine and, for their protection, some steel sheets
were arranged around the dangerous part of the machine. One
of the sheets had worked loose and was pulled into the giant
machine. Fortunately the men were not on the dangerous side;
and the sheet of steel passed right through the machine and was
crunched into a wavy shape. The workmen threw the wavy
sheet to one side and put another steel sheet into the gap near the
machine and then carried on with their jobs.

It was quite soon afterwards that Richard saw John Spencer,
master of the ironworks, walking round and checking that everything was all right. Mr Spencer got to the rail-making machine
and then Richard saw him stop and bend down to pick up some-

thing. Mr Spencer was looking at the spoiled sheet of wavy steel. Then Mr Spencer held the sheet upright and pushed one foot against the middle, trying to bend the sheet. It didn't move. For several minutes John Spencer stayed there, just looking at that steel sheet with its wavy shape. The ironmaster was thinking about the marvellous change which had actually made a steel sheet stronger. How could he make sheets like that cheaply? Could the same process be used with a machine for making railway lines? What size sheet would be the most economic to use? All sorts of questions were going through Mr Spencer's mind; and not only about production methods. The sheets would have to be useful to other people. They could be used in the building trade.

So, because of an accident, corrugated iron was made for the very first time. Mr Spencer made more sheets with corrugations in the Spencer Ironworks; and then they were galvanized to stop them rusting. At first they cost a lot of money so very few people could afford to buy them; but more and more ironworks in England began to make the new corrugated sheets and ways were found to make them by a cheaper process so that any builder could afford to use them. The sheets were sent to other countries where cheap building materials were needed which would last for a long time. The corrugated sheets were even used for such odd purposes as a giant catchment for running off the rainwater on one side of the rock of Gibraltar so that the water could be stored in the tunnel reservoirs.

Nowadays we have many materials which can be corrugated to make them stronger: aluminium, plastics, asbestos and even cardboard. One small piece of steel can be corrugated to make a strong fastener for joining together two pieces of wood.

Whenever you see corrugated material, just think that it all began with that accidental corrugation of one sheet in the Spencer Ironworks in 1843—over a hundred years ago. So sometimes an accident can be useful if someone knows how to make use of the experience.

Prayer/Thought

We can often learn from accidents if we are observant. Some of the most outstanding scientific discoveries were made by accident when the scientist was looking for something else. So not all accidents are bad.

Assembly ideas

Accidental discoveries: prehistoric man and fire; cooking by fire; Fleming and penicillin.

Activity and discussion ideas

Corrugated iron was once used for roofing many buildings in Britain but is now not so common. Why? What is used for roofing instead?

Corrugated-iron roofs are still common in Africa. Is this the best kind of roofing material for hot countries? What kind of material would be most suitable?

In what way can we learn from accidents?

5.5 Time for Repayment

It may be that there is some special wanderlust in all of us at about the age of four. At any rate, if any children are lost at the seaside, they seem to be mostly four year olds. Young Roger Lausier was just four when he was lost. He wandered along the sand dunes of Salem Beach on the Massachusetts' coast and splashed into the water. It was great fun kicking at the waves; but soon he couldn't kick them because he was so far in the sea. He tried to get back to the sands but the strong current upset his balance and he was swept away and out to sea. He would have drowned if he hadn't been spotted very quickly. A woman was swimming nearby and, racing across, she got the little boy and brought him to the shore. After a long spell of artificial respiration, Roger regained consciousness. By this time, Roger's mother had found him; so she took Roger and his rescuer to the hospital where the little boy was put in the intensive care unit.

'If I gave you everything I have,' said Roger's mother to his rescuer, 'if I gave you my house, car and life savings, it would never be enough to show my thanks for saving Roger's life.'

The rescuer, Alice Blaise, had to rush off then so she just kissed the sleeping Roger goodbye and left the hospital. Too late, Mrs Lausier realized that she had no idea of Mrs Blaise's address.

As soon as Roger was well, he came home. The next day he went to the beach and his mother was rather pleased to see that he had no fear of the sea; but he was always careful to stay near the shore line.

In the next three years, Roger learned to swim quite well. When he was a little older, what he loved was to go out with friends in a boat. For his thirteenth birthday he had a wonderful present—an inflatable raft. On the first sunny day in the holidays, Roger ran to the beach, launched his raft and paddled away in search of fish. He found a large shoal and followed them. He was so absorbed that at first he didn't notice the shout. Then he looked up and saw a woman on the beach waving her arms and shouting:

'My husband is drowning. Help him.'

At the same time, Roger could see that a man had fallen out of a speedboat. He was splashing in the helpless fashion of a non-swimmer; so Roger paddled as quickly as he could. He got there just in time to grab the man's head and hold him above water. It was hard work. The man was middle-aged and quite heavy. In addition his clothes were now sodden and increasing his weight. Roger hung on but he could feel the extra weight was swamping his light raft; and the shore line was looking further away. He was, in fact, drifting out to sea. After a long time (actually only ten minutes) Roger's arms were beginning to ache and he had a chill feeling that he would be gradually pulled off the raft into the sea. He hung on to the man's head. Every minute seemed an hour. A full thirty minutes had gone when the rescue boat came alongside and a voice said:

'You can let go now. We have him.'

But Roger couldn't let go. His arms were so cramped that they were locked on the man's head; and the rescuers had to pull them apart. Then Roger and the man were hauled into the boat.

Later in hospital, the man recovered and his wife said, 'I can't thank you enough for rescuing Bob.'

Months later, Roger was given a bronze medal for heroism by the Massachusetts Humane Society, and with it a certificate stating that he had rescued Robert Blaise—the husband of Alice Blaise—the woman who had saved *him* from drowning on that very same beach nine years before.

Incredible—but quite true.

Prayer/Thought

Many prayers include the thought that we should all be ready to give help to people in need without expecting any reward. We should always be ready to help our parents and other people without waiting to be asked.

Assembly ideas

Rescue: air; sea; floods; train; car; mountain.

Activity and discussion ideas

What are the delights of a holiday by the sea?

What are the dangers of a seaside holiday?

Should we spend more school-time on swimming and less on football and netball?

5.6 Saved by an Armband

Richard got on reasonably well with his older sister, Sally, in spite of the difference in their ages; and Sally was quite fond of Richard but she would never dream of letting him know that. She didn't mind playing with him on the days when she had very little homework to do. They had a very big garden with two swings and an area of grass beyond the flower beds. Richard often went outside just to run around on the grass and his dog loved to join in the fun. He was a little white dog with a black patch; so, of course, he was named Patch. Everybody liked Patch because he was so friendly and didn't bark very much. Patch liked all children and almost everybody; but he didn't like cats at all. If ever he saw a cat, Patch became very excited, barked and would chase the cat away. Fortunately, there were no cats living nearby so Patch didn't get much practice at cat-chasing.

One day in November, Sally was playing with Richard in the house when she heard their mother say:

'Oh dear. I must go and see old Mrs Forster before it gets too dark. I promised to mend the fuse in her house so that she can get the lights working again in her bedroom. But who is to take Patch for his walk?'

'We'll take him,' said Richard and Sally together.

'But it's late; and you know I don't like you to be out after tea without me,' said Richard's mum.

'Oh, we'll be all right,' said Sally. 'We can go along the road to the field so we don't have to cross the main road.'

'Well,' said their mother, 'don't let Patch off the lead until you are right in the field; and don't go near that main road.'

'All right,' said Sally as she went to get Patch's lead.

The two children went out of the gate with Patch eagerly leading the way and Richard holding on and telling the little dog to slow down. It looked like rain at any moment so Richard and Sally had their coats on.

'Where's your other armband?' asked Sally as she looked at Richard's coat.

'Oh, I lost it at school,' said Richard. 'It doesn't matter.'

'Oh yes it does,' said Sally. 'You know that policewoman at school said we had to wear two armbands. She told us she had been to your school and had given you the same talk.'

'Well, I've only got one,' said Richard, who was a bit annoyed about the armband because he had torn it fighting with Tony and lost it on the way home from school.

They walked on. Then it began to rain.

'It would rain,' said Richard.

'Oh, I've just thought,' said Sally. 'I've got a spare armband stitched inside my coat—just in case I lost one. Here it is. Now you can have two armbands, Richard.'

She pulled the armband over Richard's sleeve. He didn't bother to say 'thank you'. In fact, he didn't seem very pleased at all. Just then, Patch began to bark.

'It's a cat,' shouted Richard just as Patch leapt forward to chase the cat. The little dog pulled so hard that Richard lost the lead and Patch raced on across the road to chase the cat; and Richard ran into the road to try and get Patch. It was just at that moment that a car came from a side road and began to accelerate towards the dog and Richard. There was a squeal of brakes and Richard suddenly realized that he was in the bright glare of a car's headlamps; and the car's bumper was stopped at arm's length from him. The driver helped Richard to catch the dog; and Richard thought he would be told off for running into the main road. But the driver said:

'I wouldn't have seen you in time if I hadn't just caught sight of that armband on your left arm. It was very lucky.'

It was lucky, thought Richard; for that armband was the one Sally had given him. Now he knew why you needed two armbands.

Prayer/Thought
We all object to being told what to do—especially by older brothers and sisters, and even parents. But if it is for our own safety, we should always listen and follow their advice.

Assembly ideas
Road safety talk or film by Police Accident Prevention Department.

Road safety quiz using road signs.

Activity and discussion ideas
Try to make up a safety crossing song which could be used with younger children. Here is an example of a chorus which can be sung to *Clementine*:

Oh be careful, oh be careful,
Oh be careful on the road.
Stop and look. Look and listen.
Follow code as we've been told.

5.7 Fire

Martin Gray was a Jewish boy born in Poland just before World War 2. When the German army occupied Warsaw in 1939 Martin's father joined the underground Polish army. Before he left home he gave some advice to Martin:

'If the Germans catch you, think only of one thing—escape.'

Mr Gray knew that any Jewish prisoner would almost certainly be tortured and probably killed by the Germans. Martin was fifteen. He had the job of getting food for his mother and his two brothers. He became a smuggler. He smuggled bread, flour and sugar past the Germans guarding the roads into the city of Warsaw. He was caught several times, but each time he managed to escape. He never forgot his father's advice. Then in 1942, Martin and his mother and two brothers were all herded with 150 people into one cattle truck and sent to the dreaded concentration camp of Treblinka. It was a hot summer and the prisoners suffered terribly. In the camp, many prisoners died. Martin was determined to survive and escape. One day the chance came and Martin got away by crawling under a lorry which was leaving the camp. The guards never spotted him. Martin joined the Russian army and stayed with the Russians for the next three years—until the end of the war. Then he went to America. Martin liked America because he found that by working very hard he could make money quickly. He worked very hard indeed for three years and saved a lot of money. He met and married a Dutch girl called Dina. Martin decided to retire from business as an antique dealer and he and Dina went to the south of France to look for an ideal home. Dina loved the sunshine and the sea; so they went house hunting on the Mediterranean coast. Near Cannes, they found their dream home—an old farmhouse with 150 acres of land. Martin bought the place. He spent all his time reconstructing the house and making a garden and planting an orchard. They had four children—Nicole, Suzanne, Charles and Richard.

'Life is just perfect,' said Martin.

On Saturday night, 3rd October 1970, Martin was sitting in the house near an open window. He suddenly smelt the pungent odour of wood burning outside; and when he looked out, he saw that the whole hillside was ablaze and smoke filled the sky. Martin dashed outside to get his car. He got in and turned the ignition key but the engine would not turn. He shouted to Dina:

'Take all the children away from the fire. Run.'

Then Martin tried again to get the car going. The forest fire was nearer now and the thick billowing smoke made Martin's eyes water and he was coughing in the car. Still the engine refused to start so he abandoned the car and dashed over to get his motor bike; then he rode off after his family. He drove recklessly over the rough ground and nearly came off. He rode on until he came to a neighbour's house.

'Have you seen Dina and the children?' he asked.

'No,' they said.

Martin rode on to look again for his wife and children. Then, just at the bottom of a ravine, he saw a car like his. It was burned out. No one was in it so he rode on. He went on and on, but there was no sign of his family; so he returned to his burned house and then he searched the scorching ground near the burned-out car in the ravine. His wife and all four children had been killed in the fire.

The enquiry later established that the forest fire had been started by campers who had set up a picnic stove too near the dried grass and it had caught fire and spread to the dry trees. There were many other fires in France that summer, all started in a similar way.

Martin set up the Dina Gray Foundation to help to prevent children throughout France from being harmed in a forest fire; and he devotes all his time to that cause so that no family should suffer such a grievous loss ever again.

Prayer/Thought
Careless people are really selfish because they never think their behaviour can affect others. Often it is thoughtless behaviour that causes resentment and anger in people who could be our friends.

Assembly ideas
Fire safety—firemen to present film and talk to children.
Group drama with scenes showing the work of firemen—

rescuing child in smoke-filled room; cat in high tree; crash victims cut out of car.

The Great Fire of London.

Activity and discussion ideas

What things would a fireman need to learn in his training?

What are the materials which burn very easily in our homes? What things burn slowly?

What are the worst fire hazards in the home and what can be done to make things safer?

When is fire a friend?

5.8 The Three Ds

Dennis, Douglas and Daniel were three boys who lived in a city where the houses were old and some were falling down. In the street where they lived, there were houses on one side all joined together; and on the other side was a high, ugly fence of tarred wood. The three boys—Dennis, Douglas and Daniel—were known as the three Ds. They were always together after school. One evening the three Ds were playing near the tarred wooden fence when Dennis fell against a board which broke away leaving a gap just big enough for a boy to crawl through.

'Let's get in there,' said Dennis; but it was Douglas who crawled through first. Not one of the three Ds bothered to look up at the notice nailed on the fence over the hole. The notice said 'Trespassers will be prosecuted' which is, of course, another way of saying 'Keep out'.

The three boys all squeezed through the hole and looked down at the railway lines at the bottom of a steep slope. They could see the lights of a signal box and the vague outlines of oil storage tanks and railway wagons.

'Look, there's the old watchman's shed,' said Douglas. 'Let's go in there.'

The three Ds knew that the shed was no longer used by the old watchman who now had a proper brick building. They found

the shed door unlocked and went in. Inside was a table, two
chairs and cupboard with a broken door.

'Just right for our den,' said Douglas. 'We can come here
anytime. All we want is another chair; and I know where to
get that.'

They left the shed and Douglas led them to a big building
nearby which was a railway store. They stole a chair and an oil
lamp from the store and returned to the shed. It was quite late so
they all went home.

Next evening after tea, the three Ds went to the hole in the
fence under the 'Trespassers' notice and crawled through. When
they were in the shed Dennis said:

'I'll light the lamp.'

'No. I'll light it,' said Douglas. 'I got it so I'll light it.'

Douglas didn't know much about oil lamps and as he poured
in the paraffin it splashed all over the table. He struck a match and
lit the wick. A blue flame spread over the bottom of the lamp and
spurted to the floor onto some paper. The three Ds ran out of the
shed, leaving the door wide open. The nightwatchman saw the
flames thrusting through the doorway of the shed and he called
out the railway firemen who were based nearby. They quickly
put out the fire. They found all kinds of things in the shed which
had been stolen; and they found a book on the floor which had
Daniel's name on it. They soon found out about the other two
Ds and all three boys were questioned by the police. The three
Ds had never thought of the danger of that fire spreading to the
oil storage tanks. The three boys were sent away from home to a
special school.

It was years later that the three Ds left the special school to go
home again. Douglas never did get home: he took a train to
another town because he thought his father would be angry
with him and that the neighbours would point him out as the
boy who had stolen things and set fire to railway property.

Dennis went home but he decided to sulk because he thought
his dad should have lied to the policeman, and should have pretended that Dennis was not one of the three Ds. Dennis just
waited for the day when he could leave home. When he did go
away, he started stealing again; only this time he stole money.

Daniel went back to his home and said to his dad:

'Dad, I'm sorry I upset you by doing those silly things. I shall never do anything like that again. Can you help me by trying to forget it ever happened?'

'Of course I will,' said his Dad.

'That's what a family is for,' said his mother, 'to forgive and forget.'

So Daniel stayed with his family, as happy as any lad anywhere.

Prayer/Thought
We all do silly things at some time in our lives; and they may result in serious trouble. We should own up if we caused the trouble; and then try to set things straight as far as we can.

Assembly ideas
Temptation: choosing right from wrong; dares; counselling.
People who made great changes in their lives: Dick Whittington;
St Paul; Gautama the Buddha; Muhammad.
Law and order: police and the courts.

Activity and discussion ideas
Design a warning notice to keep children away from danger. What colour would be most effective?
The notice 'Trespassers will be prosecuted' is not always understood. Can you reword the notice to make its meaning quite clear?
Think of ways of preventing vandalism of telephone kiosks and schools.
Some adults think that all children get into trouble. Is this true?

5.9 No Speak the English

When Regal Morales escaped to America he thought that all his troubles were over; but he soon found out that he was wrong. Life in Cuba had been tough and the USA had always seemed like the 'Promised Land'. The Morales family were in Southern

California where jobs for unskilled workers were very few because the whole region was swamped with Mexican labourers. Regal spoke hardly any English at all; and every day he had to say:

'No entiendo el inglés,' when Americans spoke to him (meaning he couldn't understand English).

The only job that Regal got was cleaning windows. He worked hard and soon became known as a good reliable window cleaner; and he tried to improve his English by talking, as often as possible, to people passing by when he was cleaning. Most of the Americans laughed at him because his accent was so strong it was difficult to understand him. He usually laughed too, although it was not really amusing when he couldn't make himself understood. Regal cleaned windows in the town of Ventura for nearly a year before he managed to get a regular job as a school caretaker. At first he was so happy. He loved children. Unfortunately, some of the children began to tease Regal because his English was still very poor. One of the boys called Shane tried to get Regal to say something very difficult in English.

'Why you no help me?' asked Regal.

'Why you no help me?' repeated Shane maliciously. 'Why you no help me?'

After that, every time Shane saw Regal he shouted out: 'Why you no help me?' and everyone laughed.

Poor Regal no longer smiled at everyone when he struggled to put his words into good English. He was unhappy for the first time in America and he almost wished that he had never left Cuba.

Then, one day, something happened to change things. Regal was crossing the school playground and he glanced at the railway line which passed close to the school. What he saw made him run to the children in the playground shouting in a mixture of Spanish and English, warning them to get away from the railway line. Regal had seen a group of eight railway wagons which had broken away and were running towards the school. They were all tankers, filled with highly inflammable propane gas, and they looked certain to jump the track near the playground. Regal raced across and scrambled over the safety fence and leapt aboard the leading tanker. He knew that even if the tankers held on to the track they would crash into a storage depot just 650 metres away. An explosion there would affect the houses clustered near the depot. Regal hauled the wheel brake hard on, tightening his grip as the tankers surged forward. He felt the shuddering of brakes on the wheels and hoped that there would be no sparks. The depot buildings came nearer and nearer and the tankers still rolled on. At last they stopped—just twenty five metres from the depot wall.

Regal was a hero in Ventura. The railway company gave him a big cheque at a special dinner attended by all the important citizens of the town. Regal was grateful; but he was even more grateful to the children of the school. They had decided on a special present for Regal. They all agreed to teach him to speak English and Shane was the boy who told Regal what had been decided. From that day on, Regal was never teased—although he never did lose his strong accent.

Prayer/Thought

Any child who appears different in some way is often teased by other children at school. It is a cruel thing to do and often it makes the 'different' child even more different—and bad tempered too. Children from other countries need all our help in order to speak English well enough to communicate freely with everyone.

Assembly ideas

Warning words demonstrated and used in drama: CAUTION, DANGER, POISON, STEEP HILL, KEEP OUT, DO NOT TOUCH.
Group drama to demonstrate warning notices.

Activity and discussion ideas

Make up a set of safety rules for the school—some for inside and some for outside play and games.

Have you ever taken a risk? What was it?

In what ways can immigrants be helped to fit in with their new country? Is the language difficulty the worst problem?

6 SPORT

6.1 The Man Who Didn't Win

When you are competing in sporting events you have to accept that there will be one winner and it may not be you; but if you have tried your best, you have not failed if you don't come first. There are many examples of men and women in the sporting world who never gave up although they knew that they couldn't win the event in which they were competing.

One of the most outstanding stories of running happened thousands of years ago when a runner (Pheidippides) ran 150 miles (approx. 240 kilometres) in two days to bring help from Sparta to the Athenians fighting the invading Persian army at the battle of Marathon. From that time, the word Marathon has meant a long-distance race. It is one of the principal events in the modern Olympics and covers twenty six miles (approx. forty two kilometres). In the 1950s, the man who was considered to be the world's best long-distance runner was called Jim Peters. He was born in London and, like most marathon runners, he ran shorter distances in his early years—first the six miles championship and then the ten miles. Jim Peters trained every week. He managed to cut the time of the marathon so that he broke the world record not once, but twice. His speed was about $5\frac{1}{4}$ minutes for each mile—which used to be a good time for the ten-mile race. Remember that he was running twenty six miles in the marathon.

In 1952 the Olympics were held in Helsinki. The marathon started with Jim getting a good lead which he gradually increased; but at the ten-mile point he had severe cramp and was forced out of the race. Jim was bitterly disappointed, but made up his mind to win at the next Olympics to be held at Melbourne in 1956. Before that Olympics, Jim entered for the Commonwealth Games in Vancouver in 1954. The Games were similar to the Olympics and the marathon runners included some of the best in the world.

So, on a blistering hot summer's day in August, sixteen runners lined up for the marathon in Vancouver. The sun made a heat haze and the tar on the roads was melting. After the first few miles, the runners began to feel the effect of the stifling heat and one by one began to drop out until only eight were left in the race. Right in front, so far ahead that no one had a chance of catching him, was Jim Peters. But the heat was affecting Jim now. He had sweated and sweated until his body had dried out. Now it was just sheer determination which kept him on his feet; and all the time he knew that the race was just about won. He could have steadied up and slowed down but he kept going to keep his great lead from the other runners. The crowds lining the roads were not cheering so much now. Some shouted for the race to be stopped because they could see that the conditions were inhuman: the sun was beating down and the runners were moving mechanically like puppets.

Jim Peters approached the finish which, like all marathons, led back into the stadium through a tunnel. Now he was in the tunnel—dark and out of the punishing sun. He had a short steep slope up to the stadium and then the last stretch in the glaring sun again in front of the enormous crowd. They all stood up and yelled when they saw him—but not for long; for Jim Peters was staggering like a drunken man. The change into the shadow of the tunnel and then into the sunshine had upset his balance. Jim swayed and his knees gave way and he fell. He got up and forced his weary legs on again. He fell again, and again, like a punch-drunk boxer; and each time he got up and staggered on. It had taken him twelve minutes to cover half the distance from the tunnel to the finishing tape. He fell again and he began to crawl forward on knees and elbows towards the finishing line. He got up for the sixth time and then fell down in a heap and lay quite still. Ambulance men rushed on the track with a stretcher and carried him away. Jim Peters was seven hours in an oxygen tent recovering from his ordeal.

He didn't win; but people said afterwards, 'Jim Peters will be remembered as the bravest runner of all time.'

Prayer/Thought

Give us strength to face the difficult things in life. May we be brave when the need arises and may our courage never fail even when things seem hopeless.

Assembly ideas
Stories from the old Greek Olympiad—especially the origin of the Marathon.
Lilian Board and her courage in fighting against illness.

Activity and discussion ideas
Do you think there is any real difference between the attitude of athletes taking part today in international competitions and the athletes of ancient Greece?
Sponsored 'press-ups' are a very easy way of getting money for the school fund (or special gymnastics fund) and some of the money could be sent to help the British Olympic Team via the British Amateur Athletic Board. Other 'sponsoring' ideas are: running; walking; swimming.
Find out about the special Olympic Games held for handicapped people. Discuss whether you think it is a good thing.

6.2 The Water Champions

Nowadays, polio is so rare that many children have never heard of it. Poliomyelitis is its full name and it is a form of paralysis. At one time it was a frightening illness because many young people who caught it were partly paralysed and couldn't walk. Even athletes sometimes contracted polio. We have drugs to prevent the disease now.

A boy called Jon Konrads caught polio just after his family had moved to Australia from Germany. Polio victims have to take special exercise in order to keep their limbs working; and the exercises are best done in water. So Jon went swimming—which in Australia, with its warm sea, is a popular pastime. Jon recovered from polio and became such a good swimmer that he was spotted by a young swimming coach called Don Talbot. Don Talbot began to train Jon in the baths. Then he noticed that a little girl was always around and that she seemed to be following

Jon in his training lengths up and down the baths.

'Who's that kid following you?' Don Talbot asked Jon.

'She's my little sister,' said Jon.

That's how Ilsa Konrads started her training with her brother; but she was only six years old. They trained together and Don Talbot could see that Ilsa had the same build and the same swimming style as her brother. The training sessions were tough because they were not allowed to interfere with school work; and that meant training in the evenings. The actual swimming training was spread over six months of the year; and before the start they had two months of hard work limbering up. Jon's limbering up each night included 500 knee squats, 350 body presses, thirty five arm exercises and then one hour of weight lifting. Little sister Ilsa had a programme only slightly less strenuous than that of her brother. They also had to be sure of ten hours sleep every night and special meals to help strengthen their heart capacity. This heart capacity was tested occasionally on a special machine; and Jon and Ilsa, when they were in their teens, both had higher heart capacities than any swimmer ever tested on that machine.

Hard training alone doesn't make a champion, no matter how tough the training or how long. There has to be the will to win: the striving to be better and better; and this is where the brother/sister partnership really worked. They really were in partnership. If one felt tired and ready to give up, one look from the other partner was sufficient to give confidence to carry on. Each was afraid of letting the other down.

Jon at fifteen slashed the world record for 1650 yards by 30.5 seconds and knocked 23.3 seconds off the 1500 metres.

One year later, Ilsa (at fourteen) cut the women's world record for the 1650 yards by 64.3 seconds and beat the 1500 metres record by 36.7 seconds, which was faster than the men's Olympic time in the 1948 Games.

Ilsa finally took six world records. Jon took two Olympic gold medals and three world records. It was a brother and sister partnership which has never been equalled.

Prayer/Thought

We should always show courage and determination to do the

right thing; and we should treat our brother or sister as a partner in the family.

Assembly ideas
Brothers/sisters demonstrate things they do together.
Partnerships in science—the Curies; in music—Gilbert and Sullivan, John Dankworth and Cleo Laine; in sport; in films.
Unusual partnerships: Helen Keller and Anne Sullivan.

Activity and discussion ideas
Which school games give the opportunity for good partnerships?
In football, what skills can be practised in pairs?
In netball, what skills can be practised in pairs?
In shinty, what skills can be practised in pairs?
What is the best age to learn to swim?

6.3 The Name that Brought a Boy 'Back to Life'

Most people in our country have Christian names which are chosen by their parents when the child is born. The birth is registered and the registrar enters the names of the new baby with Christian names and the family name or surname. The birth certificate is made out and presented to the state school when the child is old enough to attend. At school, the child may have a name which everyone likes; or the name may be shortened, like Beth for Elizabeth or Nick for Nicholas. Some children are never known by their Christian name but are called another name or 'nickname'. Some children may have names like those of a famous person on television, so their names may be quite useful perhaps in making them popular with other children. On the other hand, if you have a strange name, other children may think it funny and tease you, so you may become bad-tempered or just lonely.

The name of a football team can make some people quite

excited. For one boy, a football-team name made an amazing difference to his life.

Martin Rohan was just nine when he was injured in a road crash. He was coming home from church with his friend Billy when a car hit the two boys as they ran across a road. Billy jumped clear and was only slightly hurt; but Martin had a broken leg, a broken collar bone and his skull was fractured and the doctors said that his brain was damaged so badly that he was likely to be dead before next day. Martin lay in a hospital bed, unable to talk, hardly moving and not looking at anyone. He did not die next day, or the next. For two months he lay on that hospital bed with everyone trying to get him to move or even to look at the people around him. He did not know his own father and mother when they came to visit him. It seemed hopeless and Martin's father was very sad. His mother was so upset that she cried every time she visited the hospital.

The next Saturday would have been a very special day for Martin because it was the Cup Final and Leeds, Martin's favourite team, were playing Chelsea. Martin's father went to the hospital on that special Saturday as usual; but this time, he carried Martin from his bed and sat him up to watch the television. Martin never seemed to be looking at the TV screen. After the band had played at Wembley, the crowd began to chant their favourite team calls: 'United! United!' Then 'Super Leeds! Super Leeds!'

Just at that moment, Martin's father felt his boy stiffen up on his knee. Martin was looking at the television picture and his face showed liveliness for the first time in two months; and for the first time he was watching something and taking an interest. When Leeds slammed in the second goal to draw 2–2 Martin actually smiled.

'Look at Martin!' said his father. 'He has come back to life.'

So the name of his favourite team made Martin begin to get better. Next day, Martin's mother came to see him in hospital and for the first time he knew her. She was so pleased. Everyone in the hospital talked to Martin about football and Leeds United; and he listened all the time. He still could not speak because of his brain injury. Every day he was a little bit better. Then when he was fit enough to travel, Martin's father took him to meet all the

94

Leeds players. Afterwards, the team sent him pictures and badges. Later on, Martin went back to school and caught up with his school work. He still cannot talk very clearly because of his brain injury; but if you ever say 'Leeds United' to him, he smiles and he will try to tell you all about his favourite team.

Prayer/Thought

It is very tempting to tease another child who has a strange name. We should put ourselves in their position and think how we would feel if we were teased. Children with strange names need good friends who see that it is the person that matters, not the name.

Assembly ideas

Short play to show how every British child is named and a birth certificate issued—Christian names and the church ceremony.

Names which can be mimed: Baker, Cook, Smith, Turner, Wright.

Christian names with meaning or story, e.g. Christopher-Offero.

Boys in school with the same Christian name, e.g. Andrew.

Girls in school with the same Christian name.

Activity and discussion ideas

Which children in school have strange names? Is there some reason for the name?

Which boy's name is liked best?

Which girl's name is liked best?

Find out if any child in the school has a nickname and how it was given. Find out from parents and grandparents any famous nicknames and how they came to be given.

6.4 The Girl on the High Trapeze

Aasia had spent nearly all her sixteen years in a children's home. Her friends at school often asked her what it was like living in a place with lots of younger children and having to share everything with so many others.

'Oh, I don't mind,' Aasia said.

But she never told them that, most of all, she missed the little things in life like mother or father just looking pleased when you had done something good at school, or just saying 'Well done' occasionally.

Aasia liked to help in the home and she was particularly good with the young children. She also helped in a gymnastics club where she was able to encourage the younger gymnasts. She wanted to teach little children but her examination results were not good enough to be accepted at college for training.

She left school and got a job in a local shop and she still continued with her gymnastics. She became very good and her trainer said that Aasia had more talent than any of the other gymnasts, and that it was a pity that Aasia spent her daytime in a shop instead of using her talent.

Then one day the big chance came for Aasia. BBC television gave her the opportunity to use her gymnastics skill in a circus. She would have to pass a test and be accepted for training as a trapeze artist. Aasia was delighted and her gym teacher was sure that Aasia would be accepted for training.

When Aasia went to the circus, the circus boss took her to the trapeze artists (two sisters) who watched as Aasia tried holds and pulls on a low trapeze, swinging near the ground. Poor Aasia found it very hard work and she had aches in muscles she never thought existed. The trapeze sisters said that they were satisfied with Aasia, and they were sure that she was strong enough; but it would be a matter of hard training if she wanted to be a circus performer.

'It will be two months of very hard work,' they said. 'Aasia, do you still want to try?'

After a long pause Aasia said, 'Yes.'

She didn't sound very sure.

Next day, Aasia started with the circus. After a couple of days she was sent up a climbing rope to the high trapeze.

'Are you all right?' one of the sisters called out.

'Yes, I think so,' said Aasia.

She left the climbing rope and clutched at the high trapeze bar and then she began to swing slowly.

'Are you all right?'

'Yes,' said Aasia.

The trapeze sisters never told Aasia that a special safety net had been erected because it was really a test to see whether she had the nerve to do the high trapeze act: and she did. They had to be quite sure about Aasia because the trapeze act is the most dangerous in the circus. Many trapeze artists have fallen to their death.

After that test, it was hard practice every day for the next seven weeks. It was just two months after joining the circus that Aasia was able to perform in public. All the children from the children's home and the house mother and her gymnastics teacher saw Aasia give a superb performance in her costume as an Eastern princess.

Next day, Aasia had to go back to her job in the warehouse of a big shop. She was not allowed to leave until her eighteenth birthday. On that day, she was asked: 'Do you want to join the circus?'

It was a big decision for a young girl to make on her own. She wanted to help people; and she particularly wished to make children happy. She thought of the circus performance and the crowd watching; and in the crowd there would be many children. What better way was there of doing something for children?

'Yes,' said Aasia. 'I want to join the circus.'

Prayer/Thought

We should be thankful for all the opportunities we have to develop mind and body at school and in other organizations like the Brownies/Cubs, Guides/Scouts. Teachers and club leaders give a lot of their time to children. Sometimes we should say 'Thank you' to a teacher or leader. It will make their work so much more rewarding.

Assembly ideas

Children's activities and interests, physical and sporting, in and outside school.

Historical flashbacks: Roman games like yo-yo, knuckle bones, gladiators, hoops, marbles, compared with present day. Similarly with other periods of history—Normans, Middle Ages—especially children's games.

Modern skills: ballet, judo, football, gymnastics.

Activity and discussion ideas

Are there any sports centres or swimming baths near the school which cater for young children?

What extra facilities are needed in the local area to give training in the skills needed in the Olympic Games? Can we afford to cover every kind of sport?

If every school had only one sport/game in its training programme for boys and girls, what should it be?

7 THE ENVIRONMENT

7.1 The Blue Whale

She was one of the largest animals in the world and she was lonely; for she had seen no other of her kind for four years. Now, nearly five years old, she was quite grown up and she wanted a mate to live with for the rest of her life. She made her strange calls over and over again. Then she listened for an answer—but none came. She was twenty five metres long—as long as a railway carriage, twice the length of many school halls, and her mass was ninety tons—which is the mass of 1000 men. Her tongue was as big as a motor car and it weighed as much as an elephant and her heart weighed as much as a horse.

The blue whale had spent every winter in the warm South Pacific Ocean; and every summer she had moved south into the waters of the Antarctic. She had mixed with other whales; but they were different—finbacks, humpbacks, and sometimes sperm whales. She listened to their sounds and understood some of them; but she knew they were not her kind; they were not blue whales.

The blue whale swam near the surface and her cries could be heard eighty kilometres away—by any other blue whale. Deeper down in the ocean, her calls could carry for 640 kilometres. The blue whale called again and again, but none of her own kind answered. She flipped up to the surface and joined a school of dolphins merrily playing in the waves. They accepted her and included her in their play. The blue whale was still lonely and she dived deeply to send her call for a mate. All that winter she swam in the Pacific. It was near the end of winter when she heard an answering call. It was one of her kind—a bull. He was 600 kilometres away when he first heard her and he immediately sent out his reply call and turned his huge body in her direction and began to swim as fast as he could. She also turned and swam towards him, each whale homing on the other's call. All night they swam under the sea; and hour by hour their calls grew louder. Then, in the early morning, they sighted each other. The bull whale was thirty metres long and she thought he looked beautiful. For two hours they played together, swimming, diving, huffing, blowing, sliding, bumping and rubbing. Then they mated.

Later that year the blue whale gave birth to her calf underwater. The baby was six metres long when he was born. The mother pushed her calf to the surface where he took his first breath. Then for six hours the mother whale taught the baby how to breathe, roll and swim. For six months the little family cruised and dived in the Pacific with the baby gaining in mass, drinking daily 900 litres of milk from his mother and putting on nearly $4\frac{1}{2}$ kilograms mass every hour—that is 100 kilograms every day. After six months the calf was fifteen metres long and he could move almost as fast as his parents. It was time to go to the Antarctic where the summer sun was beginning to melt some of the ice. The calf always travelled close to his mother for he was still a baby—and whenever there was time, mother and calf played in the water, diving deep and racing to the surface, all the time making strange whale noises of happiness.

Mother and son were playing happily together when the lookout on the whale-catcher spotted them. The crew of the ship had not seen a whale for three days and they were anxious to earn a bonus. There was an international agreement not to kill blue whales because they had been hunted almost to extinction. But who was to know what kind of whale they hunted in the lonely icy sea? The gunner captain sounded the alarm bell and in minutes the crew were all at action stations on the catcher, now heading at twenty knots for the blue whales. The bull and cow saw the black and white catcher bearing down on them and both knew what it was from previous experience. But the calf thought the catcher was something to play with—just as the captain expected; and when the calf plunged towards the ship, his mother went after him to head him off, all the time making frantic 'come back' sounds. The bull came up and tried to get between them and the catcher; then he turned away to try and draw off the catcher and so give the cow and calf chance to escape.

'Follow the cow and calf,' the gunner shouted to the helmsman. He knew that the bull would come back to protect his family. The gunner was almost near enough to get the cow in his sights. The bull dived and turned to rejoin the cow and calf. They were together again, with the calf safe between father and mother, and all three dived deep to escape the killer boat.

Deep, deep they dived and on the surface the catcher cut engine speed and waited. The whales had to rise and blow. All three broke surface together—all within range of the gunner. He sighted his harpoon gun on the cow and fired. The long, thick nylon cord flew up in a great arc; but the harpoon missed the cow and plunged into the bull. It struck deep into his back and the grenades in the harpoon nose exploded, shattering the bull's insides. He thrashed the water in agony and dived deep with the harpoon still holding and blood pouring out of his shattered body. The gunner cursed because he thought the cow would escape with the calf; but she didn't, she came to help the bull. For two hours the bull fought, with the cow and calf frantically trying to help. When the bull's great heart finally gave out, they winched him to the surface. The cow came alongside and, with her flipper, tried to pull her mate down into the safety of the sea. It was no good. She knew that he was dead; and now she must get the calf away. The heartbroken cow kept her calf close as they swam between the icebergs. They were just clearing a group of icebergs when the look-out on the catcher spotted them.

'There's the cow and calf,' he shouted and the chase was on.

One hour later, the gunner had the cow in his sights and the killer harpoon was launched. She cried out as the harpoon struck and screamed as the explosive charge shattered her guts. She thrashed to the surface and then dived. The sea was dyed with her blood. The calf kept with her making his calls but his mother could no longer hear him. She came to the surface exhausted and the calf came alongside and with his flipper tried to pull her down to the safety of the sea just as she had done with her mate. Again and again the calf rolled over and slapped his flipper on his mother's bloodstained body but it was no good; and all the time the catcher crew winched in her broken body. She blew for the last time and she blew red blood from her lungs. Then she died in a final flurry with her great tail lashing the water; and the calf still stayed alongside trying to push his dead mother down with his flipper—deep down under the sea away from the killer ship.

A seaman attached a long tube to the dead cow and air was pumped into her body so that she could be floated and left for the towing boat to pick up later. Now the harpoon had been re-loaded and the gunner got his sights on the calf. He fired just as the calf plunged deeply.

'Missed him,' said the gunner.

The calf swam right under the catcher and stayed underwater until he reached the icebergs. The catcher went back to the fac-tory ship. Three hours later, the calf went back to the body of his mother and just circled round and round blowing and nudging her with his flipper. He was still doing it when the towing boat appeared. When he saw the boat, the calf was panic-stricken and instinctively did what his father and mother had done: he went towards the boat and tried to lead the crew away from his mother. The seamen had seen it all before and they just laughed at him. A man put a steel cable around the body of the cow and then the carcase was towed towards the factory ship sixty kilo-metres away. The calf followed his dead mother, crying his sad call all the time. Then he heard the great factory ship and in fear he turned and swam away. He went on and on through the ice-bergs, calling and calling and calling. He heard no answer and perhaps he never would because so few blue whales were left in the oceans of the world.

Prayer/Thought
We think about the great blue whales, so few in number because men have killed so many. There are other kinds of whales hunted to near extinction. We all have responsibilities towards the ani-mals of the earth; and children often give more thought to the preservation of the animals than adults.

Assembly ideas
Plays based on rescue operations for animals at risk because of dam projects and flooding in South America and Africa.
Invite an RSPCA inspector to talk about his work.
Debate on blood sports.

Activity and discussion ideas
Send for details of Animals in Danger, and how you can help to

preserve nearly extinct species, from the Wildlife Youth Service, Wildlife, Wallington, Surrey.

What is meant by 'Some animals are hunted to death' (e.g. tigers, badgers, otters)?

What other creatures are in danger like the whales? Do we need to preserve all the creatures threatened with extinction? Is it possible to increase the numbers of some of the animals? How can zoos help?

7.2 Science Affects All of Us

Not long ago, a man walking alongside the River Thames in the London area saw some fish in the water and became so excited that he telephoned a newspaper office. Next day the newspaper carried quite a lengthy report about the fish. They were quite ordinary river fish, probably perch; but they made news because no fish had been seen in that stretch of the Thames for years and years. All the fish had been killed off by poisonous waste poured into the river by factories and a power plant. So when healthy fish appeared again it was welcome news to many people who were fishermen; and it was good news to other people who liked to see a clean river. Many people helped to make the Thames water clean enough for fish to flourish. The Water Board had officials checking water samples and giving advice. The power-station people changed their cooling system so that the discharge was cleaner. Several organizations in the area worried the factory management until all the factories cleaned up their discharge of waste into the river. Finally the river water was clean enough for fish. It would never be clean enough for us to drink; but at least it didn't stink any more: it was no longer polluted.

   In the time of our great-grandparents there were no organizations worrying factory management and power stations about filthy water. There was no need because pollution was not so widespread as today. We are living in a chemical age with scientists making up chemical mixtures to kill insects or weeds or make crops grow quicker. The farmers pour the chemicals on the land; and for a time, everyone is happy. The crops grow well, look healthy and give good yields. Then, too often, someone notices something unusual in the wild life on or near the farms. Perhaps not many chicks are being reared or the frogspawn is disappearing; and sometimes these changes are the result of farmers and gardeners spraying chemicals. One chemical, perhaps the best mosquito killer ever invented, had to be banned in many countries because it was thought to be too dangerous for people to use. That chemical was DDT. It was only used against insects; yet people said it would bring harm to human beings and many animals. When the plant bugs were killed by DDT the chemical stayed in their dead bodies which were eaten by larger insects which were eaten by birds, including game birds eaten by people. This is called a food chain. The creature at the end of the food chain would eat all the DDT poison from all the creatures in the earlier part of the food chain.

The work of scientists may affect the life of every child in the world because the world of the future will be altered by the work of scientists of today. It will take many years for big changes to happen; but things will be different in the lifetime of every child living today. Most scientists are trying to make the world better; but sometimes things go wrong. Unfortunately, the newspapers and television report all the bad things: they rarely report the good things. Sometimes a scientist finds out something really good and we don't even know his name. So it was with the liver-fluke mystery.

Sheep suffer from internal parasites, liver flukes, which are small worms in the liver of the sheep, so that the animal does not grow properly and a young lamb could die. All kinds of remedies were tried to cure the sheep but none was very good. The flukes could all be killed off in the sheep but they always came back. The mystery was—how? Then one scientist noticed that the worst cases of liver fluke were on wet land; and after a lot of work, he solved the mystery of how the flukes got back into the sheep after they had all been killed off in the sheep's body. The very small larval stage of the liver flukes was in the droppings of the sheep. Next, a species of amphibious snail came along and ate the larvae together with bits of vegetation. The larvae developed in the snail to the next larval stage. The sheep came back to eat the grass again and at the same time ate the snail or the droppings from the snail with the liver fluke. The liver flukes went into the sheep's stomach and then they worked their way to the sheep's liver. The scientist who solved the liver–fluke mystery had a simple remedy. He said, 'Drain all the wet pastureland and the liver fluke will disappear.' Simple, but it worked; and no one knows his name.

There are flukes which can live inside human beings. Many years ago, an American missionary doctor was working in China. Dr Barlow found out that many Chinese were suffering from illnesses caused by internal flukes. He couldn't pursue his experiments without proper equipment which he could get only in America. He wanted to take a sample of the liver flukes to America; but he was not allowed to take sick Chinese people into America because the authorities were afraid of infection. Dr Barlow found a brilliant solution. He got thirty six flukes from a patient's body, put them in a glass of water and drank it. He travelled to America with the flukes inside *his* body and there he studied the fluke and found a cure.

Prayer/Thought
Strength, courage and persistence are needed by all the doctors and scientists who work each day to make our life easier and to help those who are ill and suffering. Their results affect all of us; and we hope that they will always act responsibly in their work.

Assembly ideas
Playlets comparing the lifestyle of a child in our country and a child in a poor country in Asia or Africa.
Science for peaceful purposes: machines, chemistry, electricity, power.
The Aberfan disaster.

Activity and discussion ideas
Read passages from *Silent Spring* by Rachel Carson to stimulate discussion on using poisons like DDT—its advantage to the Third World as a mosquito killer weighed against pollution by overuse. Similarly, Paraquat appears to have no side effects

when used as a general weed killer; but it is also a dangerous poison to human beings.

What are the scientific advantages of living in this century?

Many animals are used for experiments to find out how to treat diseases in humans. Some people say it is wrong to use animals in this way, but the alternative may be to experiment on human beings. What do you think?

7.3 Noah and His Ark to the Rescue

In the Bible, Noah set sail in his ark and rescued many animals from the Flood. John Walsh was a modern Noah but he took in his boat a load of nylon stockings and hypodermic needles. The flood was in Surinam, just north of Brazil, where thousands of animals were threatened by the floodwaters of a huge new hydro-electric dam project when a large area of rain forest was slowly submerged. John Walsh was the Field Officer for the International Society for the Protection of Animals.

John made his plans and then he went out to the territory. He knew that all the animals, including snakes and rats, had some part to play in the balance of nature in the area. But when John trekked around, expecting to find animals everywhere, he had a surprise. There were plenty of insects—most of them seemed to like biting him. He saw a few sets of deer tracks; there was one dead body of a small animal he couldn't identify; there was one little toad; and that was all.

Back at headquarters, John Walsh reported to the committee of the ISPA. It didn't seem worthwhile to spend money on an expedition to rescue animals which couldn't be seen. Finally, after a long debate, the committee decided to carry on. The animals must be somewhere. It was up to John Walsh to find them.

John Walsh returned to Surinam and got some local people to help him. He was very fortunate in getting the assistance of the son of the local witchdoctor. John called him Wimpy. The natives were keen to help but they were all puzzled by the white man's interest in animal welfare. Wimpy and his friends caught animals for one purpose only—to eat.

John Walsh patiently continued his search for animals trapped by the floods. After several days tracking he rescued a few small animals. Then one particular rescue so astonished the natives that they were completely won over to the idea of conservation. It was the day when John saw Wimpy and a few others standing round something near the edge of the lake. When he walked over he could see they were surrounding a large crane. What intrigued John was that all the hunters were keeping their distance and even seemed to be afraid of the bird. When he got nearer he could see why they were frightened. There was something sticking out of the crane's bill. It was a tail—the tail of a very large snake. John strode up to the crane, grabbed the wriggling snake, and pulled. It was a long pull because, two metres later, the head of the snake appeared; and wasn't John glad when he realized that it was not poisonous! He pushed the very lively snake into a bag to be transported to a safer place. From that moment Wimpy and his friends would do anything for John. They all feared snakes: in fact they even worshipped the larger ones as gods. In the meantime they had the crane's legs tied up with a nylon stocking.

The lake was getting larger every day and John had to use a boat, just like Noah the first conservationist. Wimpy and his friends made a dug-out boat, one metre wide and nearly ten metres long.

'I don't think Noah would give it much praise,' said John, 'but it'll do.'

With the boat, John was able to rescue creatures marooned on the small islands still not covered by the rising floodwater. More boats were built to speed the rescue. They captured and transported ocelots (animals like leopards), porcupines, rats of all kinds, agoutis (animals like rabbits) and huge tortoises. One day John caught a small anteater just twenty centimetres long. He was taking a good look at her when he yelled 'Ow'. She had buried her sharp claws in his wrist. Two hours later she gave birth to a tiny baby.

Some animals were difficult to catch, especially the red howler monkeys. There was only one sure way of catching them without injury; and that was by using a rifle firing a hypodermic needle. The needle carried a drug which made the monkeys unconscious just long enough to get them to a safe place.

After eighteen months the expedition had caught and released 10,000 animals which included 2,000 sloths, 3 jaguars, 700 red brocket deer, 264 opossums, 167 snakes and lots of smaller creatures. The work was just about complete so everyone began packing up. Unfortunately, just at that time, the camp was attacked by vampire bats and John had seventeen bites. He had a virus infection which kept him in hospital for some time. As John was being driven from the camp on the long journey to the hospital he took a last look at one of the small clearings where many animals had been set free; and he stopped to look at two opossums squatting on their haunches and looking straight at the car.

Wimpy sitting just behind John said, 'Gwamba say thank you.' (Gwamba means animals.) 'Gwamba say thank you. But you no hear gwamba talk. Only God hear gwamba.'

Prayer/Thought
We are thankful for people like John Walsh who protect the animals from disasters often brought about by man himself. May we also think about our own part in conservation by letting animals live in peace whenever we can.

Assembly ideas
Music—*Captain Noah and His Floating Ark* (Record: Argo ZDA 149, Kings Singers).
Story of Noah and the Flood.
Stories of floods in England.

Activity and discussion ideas
Find out about conservation societies and agencies such as Friends of the Earth and discuss whether their ideas are feasible.

Does the United Nations Organization have any influence on world conservation?

Many people think that gorillas are dangerous animals; but zoologists say they are gentle and shy of humans. Why are gorillas thought to be dangerous? Are there any other animals wrongly labelled as dangerous?

The Jains in India respect all living things and try to conserve all living creatures, including flies and mosquitos. Is this sensible in our modern world?

Is it sensible to do nothing about the plagues of locusts which attack all vegetation in some parts of Africa where the people are already short of food?

7.4 The Butterfly Man

When Robert Goodden was quite a small boy, he was interested in living creatures. He watched the birds in the trees near his home. He watched sparrows, blackbirds, thrushes, blue tits, dunnocks, robins and many other birds. He watched other wild creatures, too. He looked at flowers and he noticed the different creatures settling on them: bees, wasps, beetles, hover flies. Of all the wild things he watched none interested him as much as the butterflies. He was fascinated by them; and he spent hours in the garden looking at the butterflies feeding with long tongues unrolled and dipping into the nectar of the flowers. He watched the white butterflies actually laying their eggs on the leaves of cabbage plants. Robert kept caterpillars in a special insect cage and he took special care to see that the caterpillars all had the kind of food they liked. He had to find out which vegetable suited each kind of caterpillar.

When he was eight years old he was taken to see a butterfly farm, and he was so impressed that he told the owner that when he left school he would work for him rearing butterflies.

Robert was sent to boarding school where his father hoped there would be other interests to take Robert's mind away from butterflies. Robert had other ideas. He began to keep butterflies in cages to try and get them to lay eggs. He got up early every morning to check his rearing cages, and the other boys, surprisingly, became interested, too. There was soon a group of very keen young entomologists. The teachers had to show some interest, so they joined the butterfly group.

Robert left school and went to work on the same butterfly

farm that he had first visited when he was a small boy. Robert's father was not very pleased. He didn't think there would be much reward for rearing butterflies, and he couldn't imagine that anyone could make a living by just selling butterfly eggs or caterpillars or even the insects. He told Robert to get a proper job and earn some money. So Robert went to Harrods in London and sold saucepans. He still kept some butterflies in the attic of the house where he lived at that time. When he finished at Harrods each day, Robert spent his spare time looking after his butterflies and developing a butterfly business which he named 'Worldwide Butterflies'.

After three years with saucepans Robert convinced his father that the only thing he wanted to do was to run a butterfly farm. So he moved to the family home with Worldwide Butterflies. A few years later he moved to the older family house, 'Compton House'. The butterfly trade prospered and he was selling butterflies normally only seen wild in hot countries—beautiful insects worth more than £100 each. Unfortunately, the old house needed more repairs than Robert could afford. How could he save the old house and still keep the butterfly farm going? The idea came to him to open Compton House to the public and make it a kind of Safari Park but not with lions or tigers. There would be just butterflies and perhaps a silk farm. To the surprise of Robert's family the venture was quite successful, with many thousands of visitors each year.

It was the first time in history that an old house had been saved by butterflies.

Prayer/Thought
Robert Goodden spends his life amongst butterflies, buying and selling and making a living. He still finds time to run a butterfly conservation society to make sure that rare species are never allowed to die out. He has taken a lead in showing responsibility for some of the beautiful creatures on earth which would disappear forever if no one cared.

Assembly ideas
Films/talks on conservation by members of local societies—naturalists.

Beauty—natural things like flowers, insects, feathers. Man-made things like plastics, aeroplanes, pictures.
Beauty in the local environment.

Activity and discussion ideas
Discuss these words: conservation, preservation, protection, pollution, progress, resources, needs, responsibility. How do these ideas affect the local environment?
In some museums there are collections of thousands of mounted butterflies. What are the arguments for and against the killing of butterflies in such numbers?
A naturalist once suggested that a child with a butterfly net and a killing bottle would learn a lot about nature. What do you think?

8 MUSIC

8.1 The Gipsy's Violin

It was while he was walking along the coast path near Withernsea that John Dunn had a strange experience. Often as he walked alone, his thoughts would dwell on the music he had been practising; for he was a world-famous violinist. He loved to go back to East Yorkshire where he was born; and on every holiday he would try to spend some time in Withernsea walking near the sea. The path wandered away from the cliff edge where the clay, undermined by the sea, was dangerous. As John Dunn turned inland, he heard, or thought he heard, a beautiful melody played on a violin. It seemed to float on the breeze and then fade away. John continued with his walk and again he heard the violin. Then he saw the gipsy encampment and guessed where the music came from. John tracked the sound to one of the older caravans and, after braving the snarling dogs, he stopped at the caravan steps and listened. A man came up, but after John had told him that he was just listening to the music, the gipsy went inside the van and the dogs slunk away. Still the music continued and John sat on the steps to listen. At last the melody stopped and an old man came out carrying a violin.

'I liked your music,' John Dunn said.

'Can you play?' asked the old gipsy.

'Why, yes,' said John.

The old gipsy handed his violin to John Dunn, who immediately tucked it into his chin and after a brief tuning, began to play the Paganini violin music from his last concert. By this time, there was a group of gipsies gathered round the stranger. They didn't look very friendly to John; but as he played, the beauty of the music made him forget that they were listening. The strange audience stood enthralled; and the sweetness of the sound seemed so much better than that from John's own expensive violins. Perhaps it was the magic and romance of the gipsy camp. John played on and on; and even the gipsy children were quiet and listened. At the end, the old gipsy thanked John and asked him to come again and play for them another time. John left the camp and walked home in a daze.

All that night John thought about the violin. He hardly slept at all. Where had the violin come from? Was it so remarkable or had it been the magic effect of the strange surroundings? Would the old gipsy sell the violin?

Next morning John again walked the path towards the gipsy camp; and when he got to the inland detour, he looked for the caravans, but he saw nothing but field and hedge. There was no sign or sound of the gipsies. At once he thought that he must have dreamed about the old gipsy and the violin. Then he noticed a line of freshly-picked wild flowers—like a message; and nearby, the scorched earth from a fire and the wheel marks of heavy vehicles. He knew that it hadn't been a dream; and the gipsies had left in a hurry. Next day, John left Withernsea for a concert tour and it was several weeks before he returned. He asked about the gipsies, but no one had seen them. Every time that John returned, he enquired about the gipsies, but people said that they wouldn't be back for seven years, as was the gipsy custom.

It was several years later that John Dunn decided to have one last search for the old gipsy. He walked the path as before and approached the field where the gipsies had camped five years before. When the painted vans came in sight, John broke into a run. Was it the same group of gipsies? As he ran, he noticed something strange: there was something wrong. Not a man, woman or child could be seen. Then a dog came from under a van and barked. Almost immediately, the door of the oldest caravan opened and a woman asked John what he wanted. John Dunn explained and asked whether the old gipsy was still alive. The gipsy woman looked hard at her visitor and said: 'Aren't you the man who played the fiddle for us when we were last here?'

'Yes,' said John. 'I've come to see the old man.'

'He was taken poorly this morning,' said the woman. 'He was talking about the last time we were here and how he loved your playing.'

The woman went inside and then came out carrying a violin case.

'He says will you play the same music again?'

John took the old fiddle from the case; his hands were shaking with excitement. He checked it carefully. He was sure now. The violin was a masterpiece. Priceless. It was a genuine Stradivarius, made by the most famous violin-maker in the world; and it was dated 1725. He tucked the violin under his chin and started to play the music of Paganini, the same music as before; but now there was just the woman and the old man. Yet John guessed that behind the closed doors of the other vans, the rest of the gipsies listened. When he finished, John looked up and saw the gipsy woman coming out of the van. Tears streaked her cheeks and he knew that the old man was dead. He had died listening to the beautiful music of the violin he had loved all his life. John went home.

Next day, John walked back to the gipsy camp. As he drew near, he could see a huge fire burning in an open space between the vans. It looked like some kind of religious rite with the gipsy men saying strange words in the gipsy language and throwing things into the flames. Then he saw the woman come out of the old man's van with the violin case. John began to run and he had a horrible premonition of what was going to happen. He flung himself forward but was just too late to stop her throwing the violin onto the fire where it burned fiercely. John saw no more because three of the men held him in a fierce grip and he waited for the blows to fall on his body. To his immense relief, he suddenly found himself free to move and he saw the woman explaining who he was to the other gipsies. She then told John that when a gipsy died, all his personal possessions had to be burned or disaster would come to them and their families. The old gipsy had wanted to give John the violin before he died; but John was just too late and the gipsy law had to be obeyed.

Prayer/Thought
We are thankful for the gift of music which adds to the happiness of the world. May we always be thankful for the delights of music which bring us so much pleasure.

Assembly ideas
Short concerts by the children with recorders and choir.

Children demonstrate musical instruments and explain about their history—recorder, violin, guitar, piano.

Activity and discussion ideas

Discuss the gipsy law about burning the dead man's possessions. Could the law have been, originally, to control disease?

Discuss the need for laws and rules. What rules are essential for school? Write out a general code of conduct for children at school.

Find out about famous violins and violin-makers.

Name every instrument in a full symphony orchestra and write a sentence about each.

Find out the five favourite 'pop tunes' in the class and the reason why they are popular. (Is it the music, the words or the group?)

8.2 Rhythm, Rhyme and Wombles

Christmas for most people in Britain is a family affair when grown-ups and children have a happy time together. The children are usually given lots of freedom and the rest of the family just smile at their noisy games. It wasn't quite like that for Marcus and Kate. They were bored just before Christmas because they had to share their house with a lot of old aunts and uncles and other relatives who were complaining all the time about the noise. Marcus and Kate were fed up with so many relations telling them not to do this and that; so when it got to Boxing Day their mother, Mrs Robertson, said, 'Let's go for a walk on the common.'

'Whoopee,' shouted Marcus as he ran out of the house towards the common.

Mrs Robertson and Kate ran after Marcus and all three were quite breathless by the time they reached the common.

'Oh,' said Kate, spluttering and still trying to breathe more easily, 'isn't it marvellous—Wombledon Common.'

'Wombledon Common,' repeated Marcus, as he fell about laughing.

'That's a marvellous name,' said Mrs Robertson.

When they got back home, Mrs Robertson went straight to her desk and began writing. She wrote two pages about an idea which had just come to her—and the idea was a children's book with the title of *The Wombles*. Mrs Robertson sent her idea to a publisher who immediately wrote back saying she could go ahead with her story. Then, for three days, Mrs Robertson wrote nonstop—thousands and thousands of words, all about those endearing little creatures the Wombles. Finally the book was printed with lots of funny drawings of the Womble characters.

The Wombles were tried out on television by the BBC and they became an instant success; and soon everyone was wombling. Thousands of children were singing the words of the Wombling Song written by Mike Batt. The first time he dressed up in a Wombles costume made by his mother and appeared in a toy shop to get some publicity, three people came. Two years later he went back to the same shop and more than 2,000 people were there to see him and the police had quite a job to control the crowd. In the next year, 23,500 people queued for hours to see a Womble burrow reproduced near Wimbledon Common. The Wombles and their songs were used, very effectively, by the Keep Britain Tidy Group. Wombling spread as far as Australia and the books and films were popular in many other countries.

Today, the litter wardens still have some work to do on the home ground of the Wombles—Wimbledon Common—because of lots of little bits of paper, secret notes written by children to their friends from the Womble burrows.

Prayer/Thought
The Wombles, in their funny way, have influenced our thoughts about the rubbish and mess that we humans leave around. Our world is 'one world' where we have a great responsibility to keep the land, sea and air clean for everyone. We should all try to make a clean world.

Assembly ideas
Examples of rhythm poetry such as 'The Daniel Jazz' by Rachel Lindsay.

Rhymes in poetry, including funny ones like 'Sink Song' by J. A. Lindon.

Nursery rhymes tapped out as rhythm on tabor then spoken as choral speech and mimed.

Songs which have had great influence—*The Marseillaise*.

Link with pollution stories.

Activity and discussion ideas

Write some new words to fit the tune of the Wombling Song.

Television advertisements often make use of rhyme and rhythm. Try to make up rhymes about litter, seat belts and safety, fire and danger, tooth decay.

Invent some little creatures like the Wombles and give them something useful to do which would help humans.

Make Womble badges and form teams of Wombles to help clear the school area of litter, and perhaps adopt an area outside the school which needs clearing regularly.

8.3 The One-boy Band

When a Royal visit is to be made to a town there is usually plenty of warning because the visit will be planned months before. That gives the town time to get ready for the special occasion. Most people like to show things at their best for the special day; and shopkeepers know that their displays will be looked at and compared, so they make a special effort with window displays. Soon, everyone gets caught up in the excitement of the Royal day. Houses are painted, gardens cleared and replanted, fences repaired; and some people say it is the only time when the council move quickly to repair the potholes in the roads.

So it was in Fowey, the little town in Cornwall so well known to holiday makers. The Queen was visiting Fowey in the summertime when the town would be full of people and the councillors thought it would be a good advertisement if all went well. They planned all kinds of entertainment for the Queen's day and arranged for lots of decorations in red, white and blue to be on show.

'We've discussed everything now except one thing,' said a councillor.

'What's that?' the others asked.

'Why, the music,' said the first councillor. 'We shall have to bring the band into it.'

That, of course, had to be discussed, because the Fowey band was very small and didn't seem quite important enough for a queen.

'We shall have to get Looe band to join ours,' said a councillor.

So it was arranged for the two bands to join together on the Queen's day.

The morning of the visit started well with brilliant sunshine and the promise of a really hot, summer's day. The last minute arrangements went smoothly and everything was prepared. The bandsmen of Looe and Fowey were all ready; and although their bandsmen's uniforms were not the same, they seemed to blend quite well when they sat down together to have a quick practice as one band. The conductor was satisfied with the practice so the bandsmen stopped playing and gave their shiny instruments a last polish before laying them in their special cases ready for action as soon as the Queen arrived.

It was now very hot. Everyone felt the heat because most of the people were in their best clothes. The bandsmen began to sweat because they wore thick uniforms which were really designed for winter. They waited and waited for the Queen. She was late—or something had delayed the visit.

'I'm so hot and thirsty, I'll never be able to blow,' said one trombone player.

'We're all thirsty,' said other bandsmen.

'Let's get a quick drink before she comes,' said one of the older men.

So all the bandsmen went to the pub nearby for a cooling drink, leaving one bandsman, the little cornet player, in charge of the instruments. The little cornet player was just ten years old; and he felt ten years older as he thought of his responsibility for the musical instruments. He picked up his own cornet just to make sure that it really was spotless.

Just at that moment the Queen arrived. The little bandsman put his cornet to his lips and played the only solo music he knew.

It was the National Anthem. All the bandsmen in the pub heard the clear notes of the cornet and they rushed out to join the lad. It was too late: the Queen had gone. The bandsmen of Fowey and Looe suffered a disappointment they would never forget for years; but the little cornet player had something to remember for the rest of his life. He was the one-boy band who played to the Queen.

Prayer/Thought
The boy cornet-player set an example to all his grown-up comrades. He acted sensibly in an emergency when so many others might have panicked. His example should inspire many children.

Assembly ideas
Story of a famous band.
Stories of composers such as Beethoven, Mozart, Schubert, Sousa.
Demonstration and talk by brass-band musicians

Activity and discussion ideas
Find out about famous brass bands of the past twenty years. Which ones were connected with a colliery?
What were 'Plantation songs' and what influence did they have on the position of slaves in America?
Find out how our national anthem, 'God Save the Queen', came to be written. Find out about other countries' national anthems, such as '*The Marseillaise*'.

9 COMMUNICATION

9.1 Success Story of Perfect Communication

Communication can be demonstrated without using spoken words, e.g. writing instructions on a mobile chalkboard, getting children to move and stop with hand signals, using a nod or shake of the head for 'yes' and 'no'.

Most of our communication is with words—we speak or we write or draw. But quite often we communicate with animals without using words at all. Think of the sheepdogs controlled Communications can be demonstrated without using spoken words, e.g. writing instructions on a mobile chalkboard, getting children to move and stop with hand signals, using a nod or shake for 'yes' and 'no'.

Most of our communication is with words—we speak or we write or draw. But quite often we communicate with animals without using words at all. Think of the sheep dogs controlled by the shepherd's whistle. There was a remarkable story on television of a chimpanzee called Washoe who was trained to use 300 words in the American sign-language of the deaf and dumb. Other remarkable communication experiments are being made with dolphins and whales. At some agricultural shows, it is possible to see some amazing communication between man and beast: one farmer rode his bull in the showring, just as you would ride a horse. Of all the animals associated with man, the horse has a special place because, by riding on his back, we have more immediate communication, so that the animal and rider become as one. Girls, especially, seem to have a way with horses. One such girl was Marion Coakes.

Marion Coakes was eighteen and just old enough to take part in senior show-jumping championships when a new championship was announced for the very first time—The Ladies World Show-Jumping Championship. Although Marion had taken part in many show-jumping competitions, no one thought she could really stand a chance against older horsewomen. But she entered for the world championship. Only her family thought that she had a chance because they knew how determined Marion was. She had been riding at the age of three—on a donkey. By the time she was ten, she was show-jumping with a pony. She was in the British Junior Team which won the European Championship in Berlin when she was fifteen.

It was when she was thirteen that the most important part of Marion's show-jumping life happened. She saw a sturdy little chestnut called Stroller. He was quite small—no more than a pony; and Stroller was for sale at £1000, which was very expensive. Marion had set her heart on having Stroller but he was only 14.2 hands high (about 1.55 metres). Mr Coakes said, 'What use is he for jumping, Marion? He's too small.'

But Marion still fancied the little horse and her father bought it; but only after Marion said that she was sure she could train Stroller for championships.

So, at eighteen, Marion was fulfilling the promise she had given her father, and Stroller was in *the* championship jump. For five years Marion had looked after Stroller—fed him, groomed and exercised him and more or less lived with him. She spent hours in his loosebox.

So, on the great day in September, Marion led Stroller onto the field for the start of the world championship. Everyone thought that she would be nervous; but Marion was so confident that she said she hadn't time to be nervous.

The event was in three parts. The first part started with the crowd all watching Marion—by far the youngest competitor— and wondering how well she would do. Marion and Stroller were in perfect communication, rising faultlessly at every fence. It was a beautiful sight which brought cheers from everyone. The second part ended with Marion and Stroller so well in the lead that only a major disaster would lose Marion the title.

The last part of the contest started off with the remaining five competitors having to cover the eighteen fences on a treacherously slippery course. The American rider Kathy Kusner on Untouchable had a clear first round and Marion had eight faults. But Marion and Stroller were so far ahead that Marion could still win, if she kept her confidence in the second round. But would she stick it? The crowd were quiet as everyone sensed the drama. Would this brilliant young rider last? Kathy Kusner and Untouchable had a clear first round and Marion had eight faults. But fog in autumn, had a clear round to win—the youngest competitor in the world, riding the smallest horse.

It only seemed right for Marion to be voted Sportswoman of the Year.

Prayer/Thought
We should try to understand other people and animals so that we may share the world in peace and harmony.

Assembly ideas
Simple dramatization of Communication through the Ages.
Short account of Punchinello followed by puppet plays by children.

Activity and discussion ideas
Try out simple science experiments to demonstrate how sound travels through the air.
Collect examples of animal communication such as tape recording of bird song; male stickleback's red chest.
Discuss whether any animal can communicate on our human level. Can dolphins understand our speech?
List the different forms of communication in use in our country.
One form of communication is cartoon, where very few words are used. Make a cartoon to teach children of your age how to train a dog.

9.2 Joey Deacon—Special Writer

Before the printing machine was invented, books were written in ink with a pen; and before that, things were written down on clay, on wax, on leather or parchment, and even on metals like copper.

The invention of the printing press made it possible for us to see anything which has ever been written. In school there may be thousands of books with millions of words printed on paper; yet they would be only a few of the books printed in the last ten years. Some of the authors of those books would say that their writing was hard work: others would say it was easy. Most of the writers could manage at least ten pages each day. The book is not finished until it has gone to a publisher, has been checked and corrected, and then the printer has to print it and put the book together. It takes a long time. How much slower if the writer only managed four lines a day instead of ten pages. That was the rate for one man called Joey Deacon. In fact, Joey didn't write at all—he couldn't. Joey worked with three special friends as a team, a quartet. They appeared on television to show how they worked. Joey 'talked' to Ernie, who had to watch Joey's face before he turned to Michael who slowly wrote it down. The corrections were made and then the script was typed out by Tom who couldn't read or write on his own. Tom had taught himself to type—one letter at a time. Joey read out the script letter by letter to Ernie who spelled out each letter to Tom who then typed it out. That was why Joey only managed to get four lines of his book down on paper each day.

Joey communicated entirely through Ernie. When he was thirty eight years old, Joey became very ill with TB and had to go into the sick ward without Ernie. He had been with Ernie for eighteen years and no one else knew what Joey was trying to say; only Ernie could understand. Joey was in the sick ward for three years, trying all day and every day to get people to understand his strange noises. But it was while Joey lay ill in bed that he was inspired to write his book. A staff nurse told Joey that a man had learned to write holding a pen in his toes. Joey had a different idea: he would write his book with Ernie, Michael and Tom. And that is just what did happen—fifteen years later.

Joey's book was all about his own life: how his mother had fallen down the stairs before Joey was born. When he was four he was taken to hospital for the first of many operations on his legs to get them to work properly.

At five he started school, but he had to leave because he couldn't talk properly and no one could understand him. Joey was a spastic. His mother understood his strange noises. She used to park his pram outside the house then she would ask him how many cars had passed. Joey would answer by blinking his eyes— once for each car. When he was six his mother died so he was looked after by Aunt Em and grandma. Some years later Joey's father married again but Joey's new stepmother died soon afterwards. Then Joey's father died and by that time Joey was living in a hospital. It was in the hospital mat shop that Joey first met Ernie who was to be his friend for many years. At first Ernie couldn't understand the noises that Joey made when trying to speak. Ernie tried very hard to learn Joey's language. Eventually he succeeded. Then the team was formed to write Joey's book: Ernie told Michael what Joey was saying; Michael slowly wrote down the words and passed the script to Tom who typed it out letter by letter.

It was truly a marvellous instance of communication by four severely handicapped people.

Prayer/Thought

We should be grateful to Joey and his friends for sharing with us something of the life of a spastic. We should always show kindness to people who are handicapped and help them whenever we can.

Assembly ideas

Lady Susan Masham and her work for other disabled people after her crippling accident.

Mary Verghese, the doctor operating from a wheelchair, mending the hands of lepers (*Take My Hands*, D. C. Wilson, Hodder).

Invite a blind or deaf and dumb person to show how they manage to communicate.

Activity and discussion ideas

Visit a newspaper printing department or make a study of a local newspaper—how the news is presented, advertisements, feature articles.

Try the 'Trenches Game'. Pass a message on by whispering.

Check with the last child to see if the original message has been distorted.

Invent a few simple deaf and dumb signs whose meanings are easy to guess. 'Hungry' may be a good starting point.

9.3 The Story of Tony

In every school there is usually one child who never seems to be good at anything; and so it was with Tony. His teacher used to say: 'Tony can't read. He won't even try to read; so he can't write and he can't do maths. He is a nuisance.'

Tony never mixed with the other children. He wouldn't talk to grown-ups unless he knew them well; and even then he would only say 'yes' or 'no' in answer to questions. The head-teacher went to see Tony and gave him an easy book to read. He couldn't read very well. He could just manage easy words—and he wasn't interested in books at all. He just looked at the book for three minutes and that was it. The headteacher said to him:

'Tony, do you like reading?'

'No,' said Tony.

'Tony, what *would* you like to do right now if you could choose anything at all?'

He could have said that he wanted to go home; or he might have said he would go to sleep; but Tony actually said: 'I want to make a bull.'

Tony's teacher knew why he said that. A few days previously, Richard had finished a model bull and it was on display. Tony thought that he could make one because he was a practical boy. In fact, all that he really liked doing was making models from paper and paste or cardboard and glue. Tony made the bull with paste and paper—layer upon layer. It was heavy and so wet that the paper bull collapsed. Poor Tony nearly cried when he saw what had happened. The teacher persuaded Tony to try again with a puppet. The teacher showed Tony how to start the puppet and then she said: 'I haven't time to tell you everything about making the puppet, so I will write it down and you will have to read it yourself.'

Tony probably got some help from another child; but he could read most of the instructions on the card to the headteacher. He finished the puppet. It wasn't very good but the teacher kept it because it was the first thing that Tony had ever finished.

One day Tony said that he wanted to write a letter. It was rather funny because he wanted to write to Susan, who was very clever; and he knew that she might laugh at his letter because he couldn't spell. With some help he managed to write a reasonable letter; and to everyone's surprise, Susan didn't laugh at Tony and she became quite friendly. Tony was good at repairing bicycles so he often helped Susan with her bike when it broke down. She helped Tony with his school work.

Something was brought to school which really did interest Tony. It was an old radio—actually a crystal set. Tony wanted to make it work. There were instructions inside the lid. Tony tried to read them but he soon realized that he couldn't read well enough. Next day, Tony began to read everything the school had about wireless, television, radar and so on. Later on, he made his own crystal set and he became quite an expert on radio operating. Tony's reading improved so much that he actually seemed to enjoy reading books for the very first time. Strangely enough, he got better at maths and other school work.

Next year, one of the farm children brought some coins to school which had been found by her father in his field. They were Roman coins and nearly 2000 years old. Tony was fascinated. He read every book in the school about the Romans. He made Roman helmets out of paper and paste; and he persuaded other children to act out a play about the Roman army.

The headteacher asked Tony one day: 'Do you like reading?' This time Tony said 'Yes.'

Tony had changed; he was no longer a nuisance. He still didn't find school work easy; but he always kept on trying hard. People liked Tony. It was a pleasure to have him in school.

Prayer/Thought

When Tony was just beginning to write well enough for teachers to read his strange spelling, he wrote a special prayer to be used in assembly. Here it is:

Thank you God for all the flowers
And thank you for the pleasant breeze
And for the sun and the rain
And for the water and the fishes.
And thank you God for all the healthy animals.

Assembly ideas
Communication: Marconi and radio pioneers; Baird and early television; work of UNESCO.

Activity and discussion ideas
Discuss the kind of pâpier-mâché or cardboard models or other craftwork which would be popular with boys and girls of your own age.

Write out simple instructions about the models or craft which could be followed by a child who is not very good at reading.

Why is reading given so much importance in school?

9.4 A Mixture of Nettles and a Fairground Organ

The two children had come to England from Syria only two days before they appeared at school. Marwah was nine and her little brother was just seven. The headteacher, Mrs Cresswell, thought they looked nice, well-behaved children when their father brought them on the first day.

'There's just one thing,' the father said. 'They cannot speak English and they have no understanding of English.'

That was a surprise because the father spoke English very well.

'Their mother does not understand English,' said the father.

'Well, we have had many other children like that some years ago; but we have had none with no English lately. We shall manage,' said Mrs Cresswell.

That first day, Rami and Marwah settled in the school fairly well, with the other children helping them to find toilets, cloakrooms and teachers. Next day was not quite so easy. That was the day of the educational visit when Rami's class were going to a farm near the school. It was decided that Rami should go with Marwah, his sister, for support.

It was a fine day. All the children were excited as they boarded the special bus to take them to Mr Byass's farm. The classteacher and Mrs Cresswell and three of the parents were all helping to supervise the loading of milk and sandwiches and the bucket of sawdust etc. The bus was just ready to leave when Mrs Cresswell suddenly said: 'Hold on a minute. I've forgotten something.' And she dashed back into the school.

'It's the nettle spray,' Mrs Cresswell said when she came back. 'I always take it when we are walking round fields, just in case anyone gets nettle rash.'

'None of our people will,' said the teacher.

In twenty minutes the bus stopped at Mr Byass's farm. The farmer was there to meet them. He loved children and he was always pleased to show them round his farm. The children liked his farm because Mr Byass kept a few horses—just to use on very wet fields where he said that tractors were too heavy; and Mr Byass had something else the children really liked.

'Don't touch the big black horse,' said Mr Byass. 'He might bite. The other horses are very gentle. You can stroke their noses; but don't try stroking old Black Ben.'

'Oh dear!' thought Mrs Cresswell. 'How can I explain all that to Rami and Marwah?'

The headteacher did her best with gestures to explain that a horse might bite. The teacher said afterwards that it was the funniest pantomime she had seen for years. Just ten minutes later, Rami was brought by his sister to Mrs Cresswell. The boy was crying. The headteacher tried to find out where he had been hurt. Rami carried on crying; and he kept rubbing his hands together and he rubbed his bare knees. Then he began to jump and dance about. Suddenly, Mrs Cresswell guessed what was wrong. Rami had walked into tall nettles when one of the horses had come near him. Rami had never seen nettles before and, of course, he didn't know about their sting. Mrs Cresswell took the anti-sting remedy from her bag and sprayed Rami's hands and knees. To the boy, it seemed like a miracle when the cooling liquid evaporated on his sore skin. He stopped crying and ran after the other children.

The children saw the sheep and the cows; then they watched the goats at milking time. After that, Mr Byass led the way into a barn and threw off the sheets covering his pride and joy—a fairground organ. The farmer started it up and the children watched as the metal replicas of instruments moved and figures danced in time to the music. All the children were fascinated and none more so than Rami who examined every moving part of the organ. He kept close to Mr Byass who showed him how every part worked.

'Come on, children. Time to go to the bus,' shouted the teacher as she began collecting her group together.

Soon they were all on the bus.

'Where's Rami?' said Mrs Cresswell.

'Not here,' said the children.

Mrs Cresswell guessed where he was—in the barn with the fairground organ, still looking at it, and with Mr Byass showing him more of its hidden wonders. Rami had experienced three things that day quite new to a boy from Syria. One was stinging nettles; another, a mechanical musical wonder—the fairground organ; and the third, the kindness of an English farmer. It was a day he would never forget.

Prayer/Thought
Children in our schools from other countries who cannot speak English need kindness and tolerance to fit in happily. We can all help by thinking what we would be like in the same position. It is always possible to communicate through kindness.

Assembly ideas
Ideas from Christian Aid literature.
Talks by immigrant parents.
Talks on Sikhism, Hinduism, Islam, Buddhism.
One world—many languages, many colours.

Activity and discussion ideas
Give a description of your best friend. Does colour of eyes and
    hair matter?
Are there any different accents amongst the children in the class?

Are the different British accents difficult to understand?

What do we mean by foreign?

What kind of things help foreign children to settle quickly in our schools?

10 SENSES

10.1 Life with Judy and Daisy (Sight)

There was a film shown on TV one Sunday called *Mandy*. It was about a baby who was completely deaf and couldn't hear any sound at all. So the little baby, Mandy, never learned to speak. She went to a special school for deaf children; and there, after a lot of hard work and worry, Mandy got the idea of speaking by blowing on a balloon and feeling the vibrations with her fingers. So she used the sense of touch to help her to speak. She learned to read people's words by looking at their faces and watching the exact movement of lips. She never heard any sound; and the film ended with Mandy speaking her first word—her own name.

It is a terrible thing to be deaf. It is dreadful to be blind—but probably to be deaf is even worse. There are people who have been blind all their lives—ever since they were babies. Children who are blind go to a special school to learn to read words by touching special print called Braille. Some blind grown-ups may be lucky and have a guide dog to help them find their way to work, shops and home.

Esther Grynwald was blind and she managed very well with a white stick. She went to work every day as a typist and tap, tapped her way along the busy streets of London. One day she thought, 'This isn't good enough. I can't just go anywhere I like. I need a dog to guide me; and I shall have a friend to talk to when I am at home.' (She lived alone in a London flat.)

So, months later, Esther went to the Guide Dog Centre and was introduced to Judy who became her guide dog. Judy stayed with Esther for eight years. She was a lovely dog who obeyed all Esther's commands such as 'right' which meant turn right; or 'left' which meant turn left. And she protected Esther against traffic on the roads. But unfortunately, Judy didn't like crowds and she hated living in London. There was something else that Judy disliked. They had to make a journey one day by train.

They got to the station quite easily with Judy leading Esther through the people on the pavements. They arrived early. Judy sat down on the platform and howled and howled and howled. She howled so much that the stationmaster came out and said, 'Is your dog ill?'

Judy was not ill—just miserable. She didn't like trains or the people rushing about on the platform. After that, Esther had to give Judy back to the Guide Dog Centre and she was sent to another blind lady who lived in a quiet place in the country.

So Esther was all alone again. She hated it and missed Judy so much she cried every night. Another thing—without her guide dog, no one bothered to talk to her. She became so ill that she had to go to a special hospital to get well enough to carry on with her job. Then, one day, a letter came from the Guide Dog Centre to say that they had a dog for her. When Esther got to the Training Centre, the Chief Trainer brought the dog they thought would suit her.

'Here's Daisy,' said the trainer.

Esther felt a soft, cuddly shape like a big teddy bear and a rough, warm tongue licked her hand. Esther was so happy she cried. After a month of training Esther went home with Daisy. As soon as she began walking to work again with a guide dog, everyone began to talk to Esther. They asked about Daisy and everyone was very friendly. Esther even went shopping in the big stores in Oxford Street—where she would never have dared venture with Judy. The stores were crowded with people but Daisy didn't mind. She went up and down in lifts and guided Esther through the crowded floors with people talking to her and children stroking her beautiful head. Daisy loved it. But when they came out of the last store, Esther could tell that something was wrong. It was so quiet. Esther guessed what it was.

'Is it foggy?' she asked.

'Can't you see? Oh, sorry. I didn't notice you were blind. Yes, it is foggy and the buses have stopped running so we have to walk home.'

'Well, I'm walking to my house,' said Esther. 'If you live near me you can tag on with us.'

So eventually twenty people all walked behind Esther holding hands. In front was Daisy, plodding on with no hestitation

across roads and along pavements. They all got safely home—
thanks to Daisy and Esther.

Prayer/Thought
Most blind people like to feel independent, so we must be careful
how we offer our help. A blind person may like a guide when
following an unfamiliar route so we could ask them if our help
is needed. Talking to blind people is a good idea because a blind
person can feel cut-off and lonely.

Assembly ideas
Invite a blind person with a guide dog to talk to the children.
Dramatize the story of Louis Braille and his invention for blind
   people.
The story of Bartimaeus.

Activity and discussion ideas
Set up an exhibition of paintings to show the beautiful things
   we see.
Some people say that when someone is blind, his other senses are
   sharper. Is this true?
Do you think that blind people should work together in work-
   shops or offices; or should they take ordinary jobs, mixing
   with sighted people?
Can you invent a written language for blind people that is
   speedier than Braille?

10.2 A Lion for the Table (Touch)

There was a time when most boys would be given a knife, perhaps as a birthday present. It might be an expensive one or a cheap
penknife. Tony was ten and his knife was an old one that had
once belonged to his father. Tony loved to carve things in wood
with his knife; in fact he was quite clever at woodcarving but his
mother was always telling him to stop it and do something use-

ful. She was afraid that Tony would practise his carving on the furniture or the door; and perhaps they would get into trouble. They didn't live in their own house: they lived in a castle. Tony's mother worked for the owner, the Duke.

One day Tony was whittling away with his knife on a piece of wood to make it into the shape of a mole when the door burst open and in came Thomas, who was the chief cook for the Duke, and also the cousin of Tony's mother.

'Cousin, I'm in trouble this time,' said Thomas excitedly.

'Why, what's wrong?' asked Tony's mother.

'It's the Duke's special hunting party tomorrow and I just can't think of anything good enough to decorate the centre of the table.'

'Oh, surely your good food will be enough to please the guests,' said Tony's mother.

'No. Not for this party. The Duke always boasts that he has the best cook and the most artistic chef in the country; and he expects me to produce something marvellous as table decoration. I don't know what to do.'

'I'm sure you will think of something,' said Tony's mother.

Neither of them noticed that Tony was listening to the conversation. On many occasions his mother had to scold Tony because he *didn't* listen—especially when he was told to do something he didn't like doing. But this was different. Tony had an idea. He followed Thomas out of the room and said:

'Thomas, I have an idea for your table decoration. Can you get me a really big lump of fresh butter?'

'Why I suppose so. What are you going to do?' asked Thomas.

'I can't tell you yet. Tomorrow I will show you.'

Thomas knew that Tony was quite artistic but he couldn't think what use butter would be for a table decoration—unless it was some new way of preserving flowers and leaves. Perhaps that was it.

Next day Tony went to work in a tiny room where he could be alone. Thomas was busy organizing the cooking for the special party dinner; but he was still worried about the table decoration. What could he do if Tony's idea didn't work? Every time he could get away from the kitchen he dashed along to the little room and asked Tony how he was getting on. Thomas had to shout because Tony refused to open the door. The hours passed until it was time for the first guests to arrive; and that was when Tony unbolted his door and came out with the result of his long, hard work. Thomas took it very carefully and walked into the dining-room where all the guests were already seated. As Thomas came in they all stared at the huge tray he was carrying. He gently set it down in the middle of the dining-table.

'Magnificent,' said one guest.

'Extraordinary,' said another.

'It is butter,' said the Duke, not quite believing that such a remarkable table decoration could be made entirely of butter.

'Oh yes,' said Thomas. 'It is carved in butter.'

On the tray was a golden lion, perfect in every detail—and all in butter.

'Congratulations, Thomas,' said the Duke's guests. 'Now we know that you are the finest cook and the most artistic chef in our country.'

'I didn't carve it,' said Thomas. 'It was Tony, my cousin's boy, who made it.'

'Remarkable,' said the Duke. 'This boy may well become one of Italy's finest sculptors. I must send him for training.'

Tony (his full name was Antonio Canova) did become one of the greatest sculptors in Italy; yet his career started with a beautiful creation which lasted just a few hours—a lion carved in butter.

Prayer/Thought

There is an old saying 'If a thing is worth doing it is worth doing well'. Many of the things we have to do may not last long but they are still worth doing well. Tony's lion was only a table decoration but he took much trouble and produced something to be proud of. It also pleased many people. We can please people in the same way by making an effort to please and do our best.

Assembly ideas

Hands of the artist—art through the ages. Musician—musical instruments and famous musicians; craftsman—potter, smith, dressmaker; writer—books and authors.

Talks/demonstrations by members of adult evening classes.
Helping hands in hospitals.

Activity and discussion ideas
Find out why there is a common dislike of touching certain
   things.
Are some people better at recognizing objects from touch than
   others? Put a few test objects in a bag to be identified by touch
   alone.

10.3 Jack Ashley (MP) (Hearing)

(*see page 16*)

11 FEAR

11.1 Peter and the Fox

Peter could never remember one single night when he went to bed in the dark. Always, from as far back as he could recall, there had been one light left on in the hall or on the landing; but when the electricity was cut off after a violent thunderstorm, for the first time his father said:

'You'll have to go to bed in the dark tonight.'

'Oh no,' said Peter.

'What's the matter? Are you afraid?' asked Dad.

'I want a light,' said Peter.

'We haven't any candles; and all the shops are closed by now,' said his mother.

'I'll stay with you for a while,' said Dad.

So Peter and his father went to the bedroom.

'Tell me a story,' said Peter.

'All right,' said his father. 'I can't read one because I can't see; so I shall have to make one up.'

'Tell me about when you were a boy,' said Peter.

'All right,' said his Dad, 'I'll tell you about when I was your age and I was afraid of the dark; but something happened. I used to think that all kinds of nasty creatures came out at night and every little squeak and sound was some animal coming to get me. My father (that's your granddad) used to be a gamekeeper before he came to live in the town; and he could never understand my fear of the dark. Then, on my birthday, my father gave me his old camera as a special extra present. It was easy to work and I was soon quite good at taking photographs. I particularly liked photographing birds and animals. Then my dad told me one day that there was a mother fox with three tiny cubs in a wood quite close to our house. I wanted to go and photograph them. But my dad said we could only see them in the very early morning. So we decided to go early the next Saturday.'

'On Saturday morning we started for the wood. It was so early that the sun had not appeared and it was still dark; in fact, it wasn't like daytime at all: it was night. We walked to the wood along a country road and then across a field. It was so quiet.

' "Listen," said my dad and we stopped quite still in the field.

'I heard a strange rasping noise and then a noise like something blowing. I had heard that noise before; but it still made me feel a bit fearful as I listened. Then I realized that it was a cow pulling the grass with its long, rough tongue and breathing heavily.

' "Can you hear the horse over by that fence?" asked my dad.

'I listened and heard the horse blowing through his nose. He must have heard us; and when we walked over he didn't make me jump because he was a friend of mine. I felt for his velvety soft nose and gently stroked him.

' "I'll bring you an apple next time," I said.

'He seemed to understand, for he just blew down his nose and then trotted off. We walked quietly to the wood. There were all kinds of whispering noises in the wood—mostly from the leaves and branches moving in the wind. We walked on. Although it was night, I could see a little and I never bumped into any trees. We stopped at a tree with a huge trunk that Dad said was an oak tree.

' "The vixen has an earth quite near. We have to wait until daylight. Then you might get a photograph."

'Just then there was a sharp crack of a piece of wood breaking.

' "Look," said Dad.

'I could just see something moving between the trees. Then another shape, and another. It was a small herd of deer. As they walked I could hear bits of wood breaking as they trod on fallen branches. Now it was getting lighter and I could see right across the clearing. Two rabbits appeared and started nibbling the grass. Suddenly one rabbit sat up and thumped the ground with his back leg. Then both rabbits hopped away. What could have scared them? I couldn't see anything unusual. Then, two minutes later, the bracken on the far side of the clearing moved and, looking straight at me, was a beautiful brown fox. It was the vixen. She stood quite still and looked as if she were sniffing the breeze. Then she moved over to our side of the clearing. The light was better now and I could see the vixen stop at a rotten log near our tree. Then one, two, three little heads peeped up from a hole in the ground and out came three fox cubs. They played around chasing and rolling over and over. I suddenly remembered my camera and got just one shot of them; but the click of the camera frightened the mother fox. She picked up the cubs by the neck one by one and took them to the hole in the ground. Just then, a dog barked in the distance.

' "That sounds like Mr Barker's dog," said my dad.

'Mr Barker was a local farmer and I knew that he didn't like foxes because he said they scared his chickens. The vixen ran to the other side of the clearing and disappeared into the trees just as Mr Barker came into sight with his dog Candy. Mr Barker was carrying a gun.

' "Have you seen that darned fox?" Mr Barker asked.

' "Yes," said Dad and he pointed in the opposite direction to the way the vixen had taken.

'Candy, however, sniffed the trail and Mr Barker was soon on the vixen's track. Minutes later there were two gunshots and I knew, somehow, that the vixen was hit. Sure enough, Mr Barker came back carrying the body of the dead fox.

' "It's a vixen," said Mr Barker, "and I think she has cubs somewhere near."

'I could see Candy sniffing around and I thought it wouldn't take her long to find the cubs' hiding place. I had an idea. I went over to the hole and sat on it. Candy came up to me, looked puzzled and then trotted away with Mr Barker.

' "Will the cubs be all right?" I asked my dad.

' "Well, we can help," said my dad. "You can bring them bits of meat for the next few days while you are on holiday—and just keep an eye on them."

'So I did—and that's how I was able to photograph the cub foxes growing up and I won the prize for the best nature photograph of the year. And another thing—I was never afraid of the dark again.'

Peter never said anything. He was fast asleep.

Prayer/Thought

Darkness is often quite frightening to young children. We can help them over their fears if we give them comfort and try to reassure them.

Assembly ideas

Mother Teresa and her Missionaries of Charity in Calcutta helped the old and seriously ill people over their fear of dying.

Ancient fears—leprosy (and Father Damien), plagues (and the plague village Eyam). Many stories can be dramatized to show that fear can be conquered.

People who help us and work at night: police, firemen, miners, power-station workers, fishermen, nurses.

Activity and discussion ideas

Why are so many children afraid of spiders? What other creatures are children afraid of? Are there any reasons for these creatures to be feared?

How can children overcome their fear of water?

What are the most frightening things to children of your age?

What can be done to calm those fears?

11.2 Changing School

Nicki ran home. It was her birthday and she knew that her mother had made her a special iced birthday cake with nine candles. She would have all her friends to tea. Even her big brother wouldn't dare to tease her today, she thought. But he did. As soon as he came in he said:

'Nicki, you'll be a JHS now.'

'What does he mean?' Nicki asked her mother.

'Oh, he means you are nine now and you will be moving to the junior high school when you go back to school after the holidays.'

'Oh,' said Nicki. She hadn't thought of that.

Next day Nicki was very thoughtful; and she looked quite sad. Her mother thought there was something wrong with her because she was usually so lively and talkative.

'What's the matter, Nicki?' asked her mother.

'Oh, nothing,' said Nicki.

It was Saturday and Nicki's brother was in the house. It was too wet to play outside.

'I know what's the matter with her,' said Nicki's brother. 'She's upset about going to the junior high school.'

'Oh no I'm not,' said Nicki.

'Oh yes you are,' said her brother.

They didn't argue any more because their mum told them to stop it and then she said: 'I think you are a little bit worried, Nicki, aren't you?'

Nicki didn't answer but her mother could see that it was true. Nicki *was* worried about the move to the junior high school; so her mother told Nicki what it would be like. She told her that the teachers were just as nice as the primary teachers; and Nicki could do many of the same things as in the primary school: there would be reading, writing, maths, painting, modelling, music and PE. There would be clubs, too, where Nicki could train for gymnastics, or drama, or needlework or learn to play a guitar.

'But I want to be with all my friends,' said Nicki.

'There is bound to be somebody you know in your group,' said her mother.

Nicki felt a lot better after that; and she felt even happier when she was told that her junior high school teacher would be Mrs Lesley because she had seen her in the primary school several times.

Next day was the first part of the holidays. It rained quite hard all day long and it was evening before Nicki was allowed out to play. She opened the door and looked out. She heard a strange noise coming from the step; and there was a very wet tiny bundle of fur. It was a kitten arching its back and looking at her with its blue eyes. It seemed to be saying, 'Take me into your warm house so that I can get dry.'

'Oh you poor puss,' said Nicki, and she picked up the little wet kitten and carried it in. There she gently dried the kitten and found a saucer for some milk. The kitten lapped hungrily. It was all black except for four white paws and a white face.

'That's better,' said Nicki as she watched the little kitten's pink tongue lapping up the milk.

Nicki thought the kitten would like to play after drinking all the milk, so she found a long piece of string and tied a ball of paper on the end. She dragged the paper ball across the floor and the kitten ran after it and pounced on the ball. They played together quite happily until Nicki's brother came in.

'Where did that kitten come from?' he asked.

Nicki told her brother how she had found the kitten on the step; and he said that someone would come to claim it and Nicki couldn't keep it. Then Mother came in and she listened to the story of the kitten.

'We shall have to find out if anyone has lost it,' said Mother.

While they were talking, the kitten was playing by itself with the paper ball and string. Even Nicki's brother had to admit that it was a good kitten and he hoped that they could keep it.

'It is such a young kitten that I don't think it has come very far,' said Mother. 'I will ask the neighbours tomorrow if they know where it came from.'

'I want to keep it,' said Nicki.

'But it might belong to another little girl,' said Mother.

Nicki hadn't thought of that.

Next morning, Nicki's mother went round to the nearby houses one by one to see if anyone had lost a pretty little kitten with white paws and a white face. When she returned home, she had with her a girl about Nicki's age.

'This is Carol,' said Mother. 'She has lost a kitten, so she has come to see if it is the one we have.'

'Oh,' said Carol. 'It is my kitty. Twink. Twink. Twink.'

The little kitten ran over to Carol and purred round her legs until Carol picked her up. Nicki felt sad that the new kitten would be taken away from her; but she cheered up when Carol told her that she was moving to the junior high school. Carol said that her new teacher would be Mrs Lesley.

'That's my new teacher,' said Nicki.

When Nicki said she had seen Mrs Lesley several times, Carol was very impressed. The two girls chatted about the new teacher and what it would be like in the junior high school; and Carol said how sorry she had been to leave all her friends behind when she moved to the new house. The two girls soon decided to be friends.

'You can share Twink with me,' said Carol. 'You can come to our house every day to play with Twink; and I will come to your house sometimes and Twink will come with me.'

And that's what they did. They both liked the junior high school when they moved; and they both had other friends as well.

Prayer/Thought

When a new pupil comes to our school we can help so much if we are friendly. When a child moves in alone it is difficult to make friends quickly; so it is in the first few weeks that we can be of most help.

Assembly ideas

Differences and similarities demonstrated and illustrated by children who have just moved from another school.

Drama in small groups all showing children moving to another school and finding new friends there.

'The Voyage of Matafu' from *The Boy Who was Afraid*, A. Sperry (Bodley Head).

Activity and discussion ideas

What is the worst part of moving to another school?

Very often children moving to a senior school are forced by the older pupils to join in a traditional game which may be somewhat rough. Is this a form of bullying?

11.3 A Kind Heart and One Tooth Less

Most children seem to go to the dentist during their school days—for fillings or extractions or to have a brace fitted to straighten their teeth. Not many children like going for treatment. The strange thing is that hardly anyone goes happily to the dentist for treatment. Yet most dentists are kind; and most people would have toothache if they didn't get dental treatment. Everyone knows how painful toothache is; and if it is not treated, your jaw could swell and you would not be able to chew your food so you would go hungry too. You would not be able to concentrate on your work and you wouldn't even feel happy playing.

When you visit the dentist there is often a pleasant waiting-room with magazines to read and usually comics too. The dentist's surgery is clean, and well equipped with the latest tools. You sit in a specially-designed chair. If the treatment is going to be painful the dentist can give a pain-killing injection or send you to sleep with gas. The dentist is a very skilled man whose training takes as long as a doctor's. Yet we still don't like going to the dentist. Rich people, poor people, old and young—they all try to avoid the dentist's surgery. Even kings and queens hope tooth-ache will go away before the dentist is needed.

Queen Elizabeth 1 had one tooth which ached terribly. Her face swelled up on one side so much that she couldn't bear to look in a mirror. She went to bed at night hoping that the tooth-ache would go away and the tooth would be better in the morning; but next day it was as bad as ever. There were important things to do with the governing of the country, and many people relied on her judgment; but she couldn't concentrate on the state business.

'Fetch the court doctor,' she ordered.

The doctor gave the Queen some special medicine—but it did no good and the toothache was still there.

'I've had enough,' said the Queen. 'The tooth will have to come out.'

Now that was not quite so easy. She couldn't have a pain-killer or gas to ease the pain of extraction because in those days there were no pain-killing drugs. There was no royal dentist either—in fact, no dentist at all. The tooth would have to be extracted by the Royal Surgeon; and he had no training at all for taking out teeth. He had no special dentist's instruments; and the extraction would have to be done with a tool like a carpenter's pincers. He would have to put his knee on the patient's chest in order to get enough leverage to pull out the bad tooth. So it was not a pleasant job in the days of Queen Elizabeth 1, 400 years ago.

Worn out by the pain and lack of sleep, the Queen waited for the surgeon. With the Queen and her attendants was Bishop Aylmer of London. He was a kind man, liked by everyone; and he was troubled by the pitiful sight of the Queen looking so worn and sad. He wondered how he could help. The surgeon came with his special forceps (like pincers) and the Queen's face showed more misery than ever.

'Your Majesty,' said Bishop Aylmer. 'I am an old man with only a few good teeth left. I will sit here and the surgeon can pull out one of my teeth to show you how easy it is.'

He sat down near the Queen. The surgeon pushed the Bishop's mouth wide open, gripped with the forceps and pulled out the tooth.

'There you are,' said the Bishop. 'I hardly felt it at all.'

So now, the Queen, feeling more confident, sat quite still whilst the Royal Surgeon pulled out her aching tooth.

Prayer/Thought
Kind thoughts are very nice; kind words are useful; but kind actions are best of all. We can be kind in all our actions if we stop to think more often how we can help other children.

Assembly ideas
Thirty two children with letter cards assembled to demonstrate the position of all the teeth in the mouth, with each card for incisor labelled 'I', canine labelled 'C', and so on—eight incisors, four canine, eight premolars and twelve molars. Each group announces the name of their tooth, its position in the mouth and its function (choral speech). Teacher discusses the function of the teeth.

Display posters showing food which is good for teeth and, separately, food which is bad for teeth.

Activity and discussion ideas
Conduct a simple survey to determine the proportion of children who have their own toothbrush and the percentage of children who brush their teeth more than once each day. Discuss the need for good brushing habits and correct method of brushing.

Find out and discuss the foods which are good and those which are bad for teeth. What are the advantages of using fluoride toothpaste? Are there any risks in putting fluoride into our common water supply? Make posters to encourage children to care for their teeth.

Write new words for familiar tunes and introduce ideas for
dental care, e.g. 'The song of the teeth' (sung to 'For the beauty
of the earth').

> For the beauty of the teeth,
> Toothpaste we use every day.
> Molars, incisors keep them clean,
> Brush them regular to keep them bright.
> *chorus* Clean them, clean them, up and down.
> Or it's the dentist down the town.
>
> Sticky foods do them no good,
> Cakes and sweets and biscuits too.
> Apples and carrots do them good,
> Big strong teeth which help us chew.
> *chorus* Clean them, clean them, up and down
> Or it's the dentist down the town.

12 NEW LIFE

12.1 The Magic of New Life

You may have seen those nature pictures on television where the film is speeded up and a little plant grows from a seed to full height in less than a minute as you watch the film. The same 'speeding up' technique has been used with flowers, grass and sometimes with insects. It is a very exciting way of showing new life and growth in plants.

Television photography of creatures is more difficult than the photography of plants because creatures move. One of the best nature films ever shown was made many years ago. For the first time, people could see all the exciting stages in the life of one special insect. A thing called a nymph, quite an ugly pond creature, crawled out of a pond, slowly up the stem of a reed and stopped near the top. Then the skin of the nymph gradually began to split open. Inside the skin, a new creature stretched and unfolded huge wings and then it took off—a beautiful dragonfly. And all dragonflies start life like that.

Another film on television was made by a man who was an expert on the photography of butterflies and moths. He reared them sometimes from eggs or sometimes from the pupa or chrysalis. He used his ciné camera to record a butterfly actually emerging from the split pupa case. You would never believe that the bedraggled, ugly creature would gradually dry out, unfold its wings and fly away as a beautiful butterfly. The photographer had even managed to photograph the tiny eggs of another butterfly just as they were actually hatching. His camera lens was so close that you could see the tiny hole in the egg shell and the little caterpillar biting its way out of the egg.

Perhaps you have seen a chick breaking out of the egg. It's a wonderful experience to see and hear. First you hear the tap, tap, tap of a tiny beak inside the egg. Then a little crack appears on one part of the shell. More tapping and a tiny hole. You can see the little beak of the baby chick. Tap, tap, tap. It seems to go on for hours; and sometimes it may be several hours before the chick breaks the egg-shell wall and rolls out, often too exhausted to move for some time. That is the most marvellous moment—the start of a new life: a life of movement and things to see and hear.

You were like that chick, quite helpless, when you started your new life outside your mother's body. When you were a baby, you were well protected; but the baby chick is not so fortunate. His enemies include cats, rats, other birds, wind and rain.

When Julie was a little girl, she found a baby bird on the ground close to the house. She came running with it and shouted, 'Daddy, Daddy. Look at this baby bird. It looks hungry. Feed it.'

Julie knew that her father had successfully reared wild rabbits, baby hedgehogs and other animals. But the bird brought in by Julie was very young—yellow on the bill, very few feathers and mostly bare skin. It was a house sparrow and very difficult to rear. Dad had to try because Julie was only three and she thought her dad could do anything with animals and birds. They made up a nest of cotton wool in an old shoe box and put it near the stove. Then Julie's father tried to feed the bird with a mixture of boiled egg and crumbs soaked in milk. The baby bird showed no interest at all. Julie's dad tried again and again. Then, remembering something about feeding the baby rabbits, he tipped up the bird and held it as it would be in a nest. The beak opened wide and he was able to drop in some food. That was the start of the feeding programme; and it meant feeding that bird every hour all the day from dawn till dusk. Fortunately it was school holidays and Julie's father was a teacher. Julie named the baby sparrow Cheep; and perhaps you can guess why. Every morning, very early, they would hear that penetrating little cry 'Cheep, cheep.'

Cheep grew bigger, stronger, and his feathers grew. He stayed in the house until he was big enough to fly. Then Julie took him outside. It was a fine day and lots of young birds were trying their wings in the garden. Cheep took off from Julie's hand and flew straight for the old apple tree. He cheeped away for a long time as he fluttered about in the tree. They saw Cheep for several days; but he never came back to be fed. He had started a new life; and they never expected to see him back.

Prayer/Thought

Rearing a young wild creature can be a marvellous experience; but it is something we should not start unless we are sure we can finish the job properly.

Assembly ideas

New things—the first wheeled vehicle, first car, a new house. Bible—In the beginning; Genesis stories.

Activity and discussion ideas

Grow plants from seeds (including large seeds such as horse chestnut).

Rear caterpillars from eggs or stick insects from eggs.

Show slides or films of chicks hatching.

Find out about all the changes in health care and the effect on child diseases in the past century.

If you could start a new life from tomorrow, what would it be like?

12.2 The Rose of Peace

Usually in September each year the new catalogues come from the rose growers. If you have ever looked at roses growing in parks or gardens you may have wondered how many different roses are grown in England—no one knows. Every year some new garden roses are developed, bringing new names to the catalogues. There are special rose growers who hybridize new roses, that is, they make new varieties. The hybridizer removes the petals and anthers from a selected flower growing on a rose bush. Then the hybridizer takes another flower from another rose bush, having perhaps a different coloured flower, and he shakes the pollen onto the pistils of the selected rose. That fertilizes the seeds which develop in the ovary (sometimes called a hip on a rose bush). The hips are collected when they are ripe and the seed is sown in a greenhouse. The tiny plants are grown as quickly as possible to see whether they are new colours or stronger than roses grown before. Thousands of seedlings may have been grown in order to get just one good rose. Then leaf buds from the new rose tree are put into special rootstocks and this is repeated many times so that the rose can be grown all over the world.

Some rose growers are quite famous; and one of the best-known growers was Monsieur Antoine Meilland, a Frenchman. He spent all his working life growing new roses. In 1941, during World War 2, M. Meilland grew a winner. It was a most beautiful rose with light yellow petals flushed with pink. It was also a very strong and healthy grower. M. Meilland thought it was the best he had ever grown. He had always promised his wife that, one day, he would name a rose after her; but it would have to be very good indeed. Unfortunately, the Germans heard about M. Meilland's special new rose and they demanded that he hand it over to them. France, at that time, was occupied by the German Army. M. Meilland had no intention of giving his new rose to the German soldiers so he thought of a neat trick. He renamed another rose seedling as his special new rose and then he sent away all the leaf buds of the real rose to the American Consulate in Lyons with instructions that he should take them to a man in Pennsylvania. The new rose buds were given a code number, 3.35.40.

M. Meilland heard no more about his special rose until more than three years later. He never forgot the date because it was the very day that Berlin was captured by the Allied Armies. On that day M. Meilland received a message to say that rose number 3.35.40 had been developed and was ready to sell in large numbers to anyone who wanted it. It would be named as he had wished, after his wife, Madame Meilland. M. Meilland was delighted, but he thought again about naming the rose after his wife. The war was over and all Europe was thinking of one thing —peace. On the very day when a truce was declared, M. Meilland made up his mind and he sent this message to America: 'Call my new rose Peace.' So that was the name given to one of the finest roses ever grown. It may be growing in your garden. If it is, it must have come from a bud which is exactly like the buds M. Meilland sent to America in World War 2.

Prayer/Thought
People like M. Meilland who spend their lives in trying to bring

beauty to our world have a job which is also their hobby. Sometimes they may have to wait for years to get one successful flower or plant; but they have the satisfaction of bringing extra happiness to many people.

Assembly ideas
Parable of the mustard seed.
Divali. Dramatize the traditional Indian story of Rama.
New life—heart and kidney transplants, heart pacemakers.
Christian Aid stories of new life to poor countries with aid to
  peasant agriculture and water wells.

Activity and discussion ideas
Look at a rose catalogue and try to think of a name for a new rose.
  Give a description to suit the name.
What is more important in a new rose—scent or colour?

12.3 The Newts that Came to School

When Richard was a small boy he had a teacher, Mr Roydon, a nice kind man who always kept some living creatures in the classroom. They had fish to look after, for the children were always given the job of looking after the creatures. The fish were not just goldfish. They included sticklebacks, perch, roach, minnow and others. Mr Roydon, every spring, brought some frog spawn which changed into tadpoles and then into frogs. There was great fun when the frogs began hopping out of the aquarium when one of the lady teachers came into the classroom. She was not amused and, in fact, she was scared of most wild creatures. She screamed when the tame mice escaped one day into her classroom. Mr Roydon also kept lizards and snakes. He never kept them for long, but always released them into the country meadows after a few weeks because he said it wasn't possible to keep them properly fit and healthy in a classroom. For the same reason, he used to take all the baby frogs to a pond.

The creatures Richard liked best were newts. He used to catch them for Mr Roydon. Richard knew the best ponds for newts and every year he would catch some.

When he was grown up, Richard became a teacher. One of the very first lessons he gave was to a class of seven-year-old boys who had just come into the junior school. It was a nature lesson about frogs and toads; but Richard soon began to talk about newts as well. He talked and drew pictures on the chalkboard. Then he said something about male and female. Everyone was quiet and he knew that he had said something strange.

'You all know what male and female are?' he asked the boys. 'What are you, male or female?'

They all wriggled, some went red in the face. Then one little boy said, 'Female'.

So then Richard had to carry on talking about 'he' and 'she'. The children were obviously very interested in newts, so he promised to bring some real live ones to show them. He knew where to get some from a big pond near the school. He went there at the end of the day with a net and a jar and sat quietly waiting. The water was quite still—no wind and not a ripple. Then something broke the surface and set up a ripple ring. Then another. Richard knew that the newts were there. Then he forgot the newts as a water hen came scudding across the water from the reeds.

'Oh dear,' he thought, 'that will frighten the newts away.'

There were no more water ripples to be seen; but just where the newts had come up for air there was a beautiful flying insect with brilliant blue wings. It was a dragonfly hovering over the water. Richard waited with the net ready. The water surface broke; so very gently Richard brought his net just under where he thought the newt would breathe and then suddenly snatched it to the surface. In the net was a newt. It was a male with a big crest on the top of its body. Perhaps there would be a female newt nearby. He tried again with the net and, sure enough, the next newt was a female.

Next day Richard took the two newts to show the boys in school. They were delighted and soon gave them names. One was called Roger and the other Susan. They kept Roger and Susan for two weeks in an aquarium with rocks and sand and weed in it to make it look like a small pond. There was a little wooden raft floating on the surface. At the end of the fortnight Richard took Roger and Susan back to the pond so that they could rear some baby newts. He never saw them again but he felt sure that Susan laid her eggs one by one on the leaves of plants under water. She would bend over each leaf to keep the egg safe from fish and other pond creatures. Later on the eggs would hatch out into newt tadpoles. The tadpoles would have gills to help them breathe under water. After about a month the newt tadpole's front legs would show (frog tadpoles grow back legs first); then another month later the back legs would show. At three months they would start breathing air so that they would have to swim to the surface of the water to breathe each time, just like their mother Susan. Just before winter the fully-grown newts would come out of the water and crawl to a hiding place on land to stay all the winter in hibernation—safe from cold frost and snow.

Prayer/Thought
The study of living creatures can be the entry to the wonderland of nature, where the curious may find excitement and interest in all living things.

Assembly ideas
Spring—new life from a dead world.
John Clare and his poems.
Invite a mother to bring her baby to school and talk about baby care.

Activity and discussion ideas
What are the most important things for a young mother to know about how to care for her new baby?
In what ways are human babies like animal babies?
If you had the choice of rearing one young animal, bird or insect, which would it be and why?

13 ANIMALS

13.1 The Elephant Who Didn't Forget

Fabian Redwood lived in America. He was slowly reading his newspaper. He was seventy six and retired so he was in no hurry and he read everything—even the small news items. He began to read the advertisements; and it was then that he saw that a circus was coming to town. Well, that was interesting because Fabian Redwood used to have his own circus. Then he read about the circus star, Modoc.

'Surely not old Modoc? My Modoc?' said Fabian, talking to himself. (Old people sometimes do that.) And then his thoughts went back to the days when he was young—when he was a circus trainer and Modoc was his special elephant. Why, it must be fifty years ago when he had said goodbye to Modoc and had left the circus to start his own animal show. Could it be the same elephant? There was only one way to find out.

Fabian Redwood hurried to the fairground as fast as his arthritis would let him. There he explained to the circus people about Modoc.

'Oh, we can't let you go near that elephant,' they said. 'She is quite nasty with strangers.'

'But I'm not a stranger,' said Fabian.

'Of course you are,' said the circus boss. 'Even if she is the same Modoc, you are talking about what happened fifty years ago. She would never remember you.'

Fabian looked so miserable that, just to humour him, the animal trainer went to bring Modoc into the ring. Fabian waited in the ringside seats. He waited and wondered. If it was Modoc, would she recognize him? When she had last seen him he had been a young man of twenty four. Now he was a wizened, crippled seventy six year old. Modoc herself was quite old; in fact she was two years older than Fabian.

Just then the elephant walked in. She walked round the ring

and stopped in front of the old man. Then she gave a squeal and Fabian called out, 'Modoc! Trunk up, Modoc.'

The old elephant reared up on her hind legs and flung her trunk high in the air. Then she came down and ambled up to the seats, seized Fabian in her trunk and raised him to eye level so that she could have a good look at him. As she lowered Fabian to the ground, all the circus folk applauded. There were tears in Fabian's eyes although he had never doubted that the elephant would remember him. Then he noticed some dark blotches on Modoc's trunk and ears. The circus people told him that they were old burn marks from a circus fire in Connecticut, when Modoc helped to drag cageloads of terrified animals to safety. That was when she was forty eight years old. Later on she had appeared in several Hollywood films, including *Daktari*.

As Modoc went back to her stable with her trunk wrapped round Fabian's arm, the circus boss said, 'An animal does what her trainer wants out of love or respect. Look at them now and think how they both have changed in half a century. Yet they still knew each other.'

Prayer/Thought
We should always show respect for animals and be kind to them. The people who care for and train animals find that the best results are from training methods combined with kindness. We should remember that when we are dealing with animals.

Assembly ideas
Conservation of animals such as tiger, elephant, rhinoceros.
The RSPB and young ornithologists.
Talk by RSPCA official.

Activity and discussion ideas
Make silhouettes of birds for quick recognition.
Cut out large pictures of animals and write about the animal on one side.
Some people say that it is cruel to have animals in a circus. Discuss this.
How can we preserve and protect those animals in danger of extinction?

Find out about working elephants in the forests of Burma. Read stories about 'Elephant Bill'.

13.2 Follow the Leader

Whenever we think of great leaders we think of people, but sometimes a leader can be an animal.

In the early part of World War 2, Burma was partly overrun by the Japanese Army, but there were still British people working in that country. Burma has huge forests of teak which is a strong wood used for bridge building and road construction. The timber was cut down in the forests and the logs were pulled out by elephants. The biggest elephant camp was commanded by Lieutenant Colonel J. H. Williams, known as 'Elephant Bill'. In March 1944, a senior British Army Officer ordered Colonel Williams to move all his working elephants out of Burma into Assam, which was due west of their camp and the nearest part of India. It was just a matter of moving from one valley into another valley, but there was one problem: there were five mountain ranges in the way and the mountains were nearly 2000 metres high.

It took five days to get all the elephant teams back from the forest camps and ready for the great march. There were forty five elephants, ninety elephant riders called oozies, forty Burmese soldiers and sixty four refugee women and children. They started on the 5th April 1944 and Elephant Bill rode ahead to watch the party from a small hill. From his position he said that the elephants were strung out like a long line of moles followed by a trail of black ants. They were so far apart that he thought the leader would arrive at their destination before the last one had started.

After two days of hard marching the refugee women and children were exhausted and some of the elephants with the heaviest loads were too worn out to carry any more so they had to be unloaded and their things were shared out amongst the other elephants. They were now in the higher ranges of hills and a number of the refugees were ill with pneumonia and malaria. It rained heavily every night and the women begged Elephant Bill to stop and let them rest for a day.

'I'm sorry,' he said, 'but we have to push on. The Japanese are too close.'

So they marched on, starting at dawn each day and not stopping till five in the afternoon. At that point on the march the children had mastered the art of riding on the elephants, so they were not so fatigued by the long marches, and their mothers went ahead of the party to cut down the bamboos and clear a path for the elephants to follow. Then, to everyone's surprise, Elephant Bill called a halt. They soon found the reason when the following elephants caught up with the leader. In front of them was a sheer rock cliff, more than 100 metres high. It looked impassable by man and impossible by elephant. They made camp. For two days Elephant Bill explored the cliff face looking for a route. Suddenly he shouted:

'Look! There's a possible track here!'

It looked like a track of some kind—suitable for goats, not elephants.

'We'll dig it out and widen it,' said Elephant Bill.

And they did. The rock was sandstone and so they were able to hack out rough steps, but there were still two very dangerous parts where a ledge, less than a metre wide, looked as if it would collapse under the weight of an elephant.

'We'll have to try it,' said Elephant Bill. 'We need one elephant to take the lead.'

He chose Bandoola, who was now forty five years old and a magnificent tusker. If he kept his nerve, the other elephants would follow, but if Bandoola failed, they would be stranded and the Japanese Army would capture them all. Elephant Bill walked ahead and took up a position just beyond the most dangerous ledge so that he could see Bandoola. As he stood waiting he could hear the gunfire from the advancing Japanese Army. He looked towards the small steps they had cut in the sandstone, just big enough to take the elephants' feet one by one. An hour passed. Then another hour. It looked like failure and a Japanese Prisoner of War camp. Then Bandoola's head and tusks appeared round the corner. The oozie on his back appeared to be directing

Bandoola, telling him where to place each foot. The path was so steep at that point that Bandoola seemed to be standing nearly upright on his hind legs. Would he make it? It was a full minute before Elephant Bill realized that Bandoola had done it. He was now over the worst and steadily pushing on to the top of the cliff. All the other elephants followed. There were no accidents. All reached the top safely. After another nine days march they reached the camp in Assam.

So ended the greatest elephant trek since Hannibal crossed the Alps. There was no great victory parade for Colonel Williams, but there was a feeling of pride as he watched forty five elephants and nearly 200 adults and children settle down for the night in safety amongst friends.

He was a great leader: Bandoola.

Prayer/Thought
Many of us follow the example of a good leader; and intelligent animals often do so. When we are able to choose good leaders they should be wise and brave and fair.

Assembly ideas
RSPCA letters used separately by children in group demonstrations.
Respect—e.g. dignity of animals.
Saving species in zoos by breeding and sending back to country of origin.
Preserving—game parks and conservation.
Caring—anti otter hunting. Caring for pets.
Animals—farm and wild.
Tame animals helpful to man: elephant, dog, camel, donkey, horse etc.

Activity and discussion ideas
Topic study of animals used by man.
Make a collection of nursery rhymes which are about animals. e.g. Baa, baa, black sheep.
Which animals do you think are the most intelligent? Give reasons for your choice.

13.3 Corrie the Brave Deer

If you have ever been to Scotland you may have been lucky enough to see some of the wild deer; or perhaps you may have seen a herd in a zoo. There are hundreds and hundreds of deer living in Scotland; but they are very shy and they hide from us in the day-time. Two forest rangers were once watching an old stag and a newborn calf deer. The rangers were wondering where the mother deer was. She came into view and at once they could see that she was hurt. She had a gaping wound in her side and, as they watched, the mother deer collapsed and lay still on the ground. At that moment, the labrador dog owned by one of the rangers began barking excitedly and the old stag was frightened and galloped away, leaving the baby deer on its own. The little deer ran around and round, its mother making little crying noises.

'It'll never live through to morning,' said one of the rangers, Mr McFaddyan.

'No, I'm sure it won't,' said Mr McEwen, the other ranger.

'Help me to catch it,' said Mr McFaddyan. 'I'll take it home. Fiona and Alastaire will look after it.'

It didn't take long to catch the frightened little deer; and Mr McFaddyan carried it to his house in the woods. When Fiona saw the baby animal she said: 'Oh, what a lovely present.'

It was her birthday next day; so she thought that her father had brought the baby deer specially for her birthday present. Her father began to explain about the mother deer, but he didn't finish because Alastaire ran into the kitchen shouting: 'Dad, where's the baby deer?'

Soon the children were busy calming the baby and making friends. Then they had to get it to drink milk from a baby's feeding-bottle.

'We must give him a name,' said Fiona.

'Yes,' said Alastaire, 'let's call him Corrie.'

That was the name of the place where they lived—Corrie Rou.

So Corrie grew up with the children and two other pets—a Pekinese dog called Chang and a labrador named Bongo. The three animals used to play together in the house where, on windy wet days, they ran all over skidding and sliding on the polished floors. They had great fun; but Mrs McFaddyan was not very pleased when she found all her mats kicked up and sometimes things were broken.

'That stupid Corrie,' she would say. 'Why ever did we bring him into the house. He is a nuisance.'

But Mrs McFaddyan always calmed down later; and then she would have to admit that she really liked Corrie.

The baby deer grew bigger until he really was too big for the house; so he had to move into the stable outside. Corrie had a nice red collar with brass studs. He was so fond of the children that he cried every time they left the house without him. He tried to follow them everywhere; but he was not allowed to go to school. As soon as Alastaire and Fiona were back from school each day, they would let Corrie out of the stable and he would play with them. One of the games that Corrie liked was to stand up on his hind legs and box just like a boxer. His little hoofs were quite sharp and Alastaire got a badly-cut forehead; so Alastaire's mother said: 'No more boxing with Corrie. It has to stop before somebody gets badly hurt.'

Corrie still played games. He used to chase the postman. He didn't like anyone in uniform coming to the house. Mrs McFaddyan said that Corrie was becoming a nuisance now that he was bigger; and Fiona and Alastaire knew what she would say if anything really bad happened.

Then one day something did happen. Mrs McFaddyan heard the dogs barking fiercely while she was cleaning up in the bedroom. She rushed to the window. She could see Bongo and Chang barking away; and Corrie was rearing up on his hind legs, dangerously close to the baby lying on a rug in the sun. Mrs McFaddyan thought, 'Corrie will hit the baby'; and just at that moment there was a swish of wings as an eagle dived over the baby and Corrie did his boxing act to keep the eagle away. Mrs McFaddyan realized that the brave little deer was defending the baby against the eagle.

Never again did she grumble about Corrie or say that he was a nuisance.

Prayer/Thought

We share the earth with all kinds of wild creatures; and we are responsible for many of their lives and deaths. Kindness to an animal may cost us very little; but in return we may gain a great deal.

Assembly ideas
Man and animal friendships: Androcles and the lion; Dick Whittington and his cat; *Born Free*, Joy Adamson, (Collins). Debate on blood sports.

Activity and discussion ideas
Is it possible to train a pet deer on similar lines to a dog or horse? If so, how could it be done?

Is it a good idea to treat wild animals as pets? What about lions which may grow up big and savage?

As a nation, we think we are kind to pets. Are we just as kind to wild animals?

13.4 Zoos without Bars

When you visit a zoo like London Zoo or Flamingo Park you may be disappointed because some animals in the large outside enclosures cannot be seen. They may be under cover in long grass in summer or in wooden shelters in the winter. The zoo has made enclosures to suit the animals rather than the human visitors. But it wasn't always so. Until a few years ago, the zoos usually had lions, tigers, elephants, giraffes all in separate cages. They often looked healthy but they always seemed restless. There was a boy called George Mottershead who had very strong views about animals kept in cages. When his parents took him to a zoo for the first time, they thought there was something wrong with young George. They thought he was ill because he hardly said a word all day and he looked moody. In fact, when the family got back home, Mrs Mottershead gave George a dose of medicine. Then George ran out into the garden to look at his pets. He had birds in an aviary, lizards and beetles in large tanks and Plymouth Rock chickens in a large hen house. He could see that they all had plenty of space to move about and all were in clean surroundings. Then he knew what had bothered him all day: that zoo had all the animals in little prisons without enough room to move about freely. George ran back into the house and with all the impetuosity of an eight year old, he said to his parents: 'When I'm old enough I shall have a proper zoo where all the animals will be free to move; and they won't be in cages at all.'

It was a long time before George was able to do anything more about his special kind of zoo. When he was grown up and married he had a nursery where he grew and sold plants and flowers. Everyone called him Mott. One day, Mott bought a chimpanzee called Mary. She was a marvellous pet and Mott decided to get her some friends, so he bought some rare monkeys. His next idea was to move his animals and his family to a new place at Chester. So Mott, his wife and his elder daughter Muriel were soon hard at work making buildings for the monkeys in their new place which had nine acres of land. He had another helper to mix the mortar, carry timber, nails and tools, and even lay some of the bricks. It was Mary the chimp. The enclosures were all finished ready for the animals but then Mott ran into trouble. The people who lived nearby objected to a zoo and said they didn't want dirty wild animals near their homes. Mott had to get permission from the Minister of Health to go ahead with his private zoo. Then he was able to announce a grand opening with his few animals and the special attraction of two black bears called Adam and Eve. Unfortunately, hardly anyone came to the grand opening so Mott knew he would have difficulty in keeping his animals without money to pay for food. Then he had an idea. He made his zoo into a non-profit-making society and he found enough supporters to keep going. Mott wanted to try out his boyhood idea of getting even the big cats into open enclosures rather than confined to barred cages; but he was unable to get started because the Second World War began and all dangerous animals had to be kept in barred cages in case of panic with air raids and bombing attacks. Zoos all over Britain had to close down because they couldn't afford to feed and look after the expensive animals.

Mott refused to close down and then he had another bright idea. He appealed to children and their parents to adopt an animal. Monkeys and smaller animals were a shilling a week, chimps were five shillings, lions ten shillings and bears a pound. The response from children and adults all over Britain was so great that Mott made his first-ever profit from the zoo. Another thing happened too. All over the country, as the zoos closed down, they sent some of their animals to Chester for Mott and his helpers to look after. When the war ended, Mott said that he would try to get all his animals enough room to move freely.

'I'll get those lions and tigers away from bars,' he said.

Mott started with the lions. He built a chain-link fence around a bit of land with trees and shrubs already growing. Then he set free the lions inside the chain-link fence. Mott and his helpers watched and waited. From their set faces, Mott could see what *they* thought about the wire fence. Mott waited and watched the lions anxiously. The cubs all settled in immediately and began to play around the bushes and rocks; but the older lions were obviously suspicious. They walked, stiff-legged, round the peri-meter of the fence and snarled at every tree and even snarled at the posts holding the fence. It was the same next day, and the next. In fact it was a week before the adult lions settled down; but after that they were all right. So Mott moved the tigers into open land behind a similar chain-link fence. Zoos all over the world heard of Mott's theory of keeping savage big cats in open areas. They were finally convinced when something happened to Mott's zoo which could have been a calamity. A large elm tree fell on the tiger fence during a storm. The tigers could have escaped quite easily; but all they did was to sniff around the gap in the fence rather suspiciously; then they snarled at the broken fence until their keeper came to repair it. They never attempted to escape. So Mott proved that his theory was practicable—he had a zoo without bars even for dangerous animals.

Now, all over the world, zoos have been built or rebuilt along the lines suggested by George Mottershead.

If you ever go to Chester, don't miss Chester Zoo—that is Mott's Zoo—first started by Mott and his family, including Mary the chimp.

Prayer/Thought

If we confine a wild animal in a cage, at home for our own

pleasure, or in a zoo, we take on the responsibility of caring for that animal and giving it as natural an existence as we can.

Assembly ideas
Children to present their own ideas on a favourite animal.
Animals in books—*Tarka the Otter, Watership Down, Black Beauty, Aesop's Fables.*
Zoo animals and their countries of origin.

Activity and discussion ideas
Visit to a zoo as part of a topic on animals.
In some parts of Africa the hunting of elephants was stopped in the game parks; but now the herds have increased so much that other wild life is menaced. Can game areas be used for the benefit of just one kind of animal? What animals in Britain need protection, perhaps in game areas?

14 PETS

14.1 Scruffy

The story about the good Samaritan is very well known. Jesus told that story to get his audience to see that your neighbour can be anyone—friend or foreigner—who is in need of help; and you can be a neighbour by helping anyone in trouble.

Here is a story, a modern one, about someone who needed a neighbour.

At first, the little puppy was a delightful bundle of black and white fur; but as he grew older, he began to fit his name of Scruffy. He had a long, ever-wagging tail with a plume of wispy grey hair. His black ears hung down over a very whiskery face. He was the sort of dog which is difficult to describe. The only thing you could really say about him was that he was absolutely devoted to Sarah and Timothy. Unfortunately, the children's mother didn't like Scruffy. She didn't like any dogs really; but Dad had brought the little pup home from work as a present for the two children.

'That wretched dog has been sleeping in the armchair again,' shouted Mother. 'It's covered with dog hairs. I don't know why we keep that animal.'

'Oh Mum,' said Sarah, 'he doesn't understand yet about chairs. I'll train him.'

'He doesn't understand about toilets either,' said Mother. 'I'm fed up with him.'

The front door slammed and Dad was home from work; and just at that moment, Scruffy decided to use the dining-room carpet as a lavatory.

'Look at that,' shrieked Mother. 'Get out, you brute!' and she kicked the little dog out of the house and into the street.

Poor Scruffy was bewildered. He didn't understand about using the garden or field as a lavatory because no one had bothered to train him. He sat down on the pavement. Then he noticed a big dog walking down the street some distance away;

so Scruffy trotted after the other dog. The big dog went on and on until Scruffy was quite tired and sat down for a rest. When he trotted on again, the big dog had disappeared.

It was the delicious smell which first attracted Scruffy to the big, meaty bone near the hedge. He trotted over, sniffed it appreciatively and began to gnaw the bone. He had taken one more bite when a white terrier bounded out of the hedge and jumped at Scruffy. Before the little dog could move, the terrier had bitten him on the front paw—enough to make him squeal with pain and rush away on his three sound legs as fast as he could. Scruffy ran into the road and was hit a glancing blow by a bicycle. The cyclist, a kind man, stopped to see if the little dog was injured; but Scruffy was now so frightened that he ran away as fast as his three legs could carry him.

That night, Scruffy slept in a large new drainage pipe at the side of a new road. In the morning he crept out of the pipe and was immediately attacked by a bad-tempered dog who treated the pipe as his territory. Poor Scruffy ran until he was quite exhausted and then he collapsed in a heap on the steps of an old cottage in a part of the town where the buildings were being demolished.

A few minutes later, a man walked past the cottage on the way to the railway station. He glanced briefly at the dog stretched out on the steps; then he looked at his watch and rushed on to catch his train.

Next, a woman saw the dog and knew that it was seriously hurt. She thought, 'Oh, I can't stand injured animals. Besides, it's a dog, and a sick dog might bite me and give me some disease.' She hurried on.

The next to see Scruffy was not a person at all: it was a big, friendly sheepdog called Mac. He came over to Scruffy and sat down on the steps and licked the little dog's injured leg. After a while, Mac began to bark. It was Jenny who opened the door to see what all the noise was about.

'Oh, you poor little thing,' she said when she saw Scruffy.

Jenny picked up the little dog and carried him into the house whilst Mac went on to his home in the next street.

'Mum,' shouted Jenny to her mother upstairs. 'Look what I've found on the doorstep.'

When Jenny's mother came down she could see at once that the little dog was very ill.

'We'll have to get him to a vet,' said Jenny's mother.

Jenny carried Scruffy to the vet where a broken bone was set and, after an injection, the little dog was carried back to the cottage. Scruffy lay on a blanket near the stove all day until Jenny came home from school. Then, for the first time, his long grey tail moved—just once. Jenny could see that he was very weak so, after tea, she sat with Scruffy on the floor. It was hours later when Jenny's father heard her shout.

'Dad, I can't feel his heart beat. I think it has stopped.'

Jenny's father knelt down and massaged the dog's heart as Jenny held the little animal on her lap. They had almost given up hope when there was a tiny movement and a little whimper; and then Scruffy's big brown eyes opened and looked up at Jenny and a pink tongue licked her hand.

Next day the vet called.

'Will he be all right?' asked Jenny.

'He needs lots of love and kindness; and I don't know anyone who'll give him more than you will. He'll get better.'

Prayer/Thought

May we be thoughtful and kind like the good Samaritan and help *anyone* in need, so following the advice of Jesus to help our neighbour.

Assembly ideas

Simple dramatization of The Good Samaritan story, with children to explain 'who is my neighbour?'.

Dr Barnardo and his work with children 'neighbours'.

The work of Christian Aid and Oxfam in the developing countries.

Activity and discussion ideas

Contact the local branch of Age Concern to determine the needs of local old folk. Children could arrange straight collection or activities to get money for local Age Concern.

Write to Help the Aged, 8–10 Denman Street, London W1A 2AP for details of Education Pack.

Arrange a concert for old age pensioners.

Write a story about helping a friend in trouble, or about someone helping an animal in need.

Make a picture and describe a simple aid which an old person could use in the house (perhaps in the window) to warn the neighbours that their help is needed quickly.

14.2 The Furry Fire Alarm

It was a miserable wet evening and even the television programmes were having an off day because there was nothing on that Anthony wanted to watch.

'What can I do, Mum?' Anthony asked his mother.

'You could read some of those books you never open,' said his mother. 'Then perhaps you'll be a bit better at school.'

'Oh, no!' said Anthony.

Just then he heard, or thought he heard, a faint sound outside—quite different from the patter and gurgle of the rain. Anthony went near to the kitchen door and listened. It was a strange noise like a cat with a sore throat. He opened the door and looked, astonished, at the little creature that stalked in.

'Mum, come and look! We've got a visitor.'

When Anthony's mother came to see who the visitor was, she was quite surprised to find a bedraggled, fawn coloured kitten with strange blue eyes and sharp little ears.

'Why, it's a Siamese kitten. Where did he come from?'

Anthony didn't say anything. He was busy picking up the wet kitten and looking for a towel to dry it.

'Don't use that towel,' said his mother. 'I'll find an old one.'

Anthony didn't say anything. He was busy picking up the some food, for he was quite convinced that the little kitten was starving.

'We shall have to find who owns this kitten,' said Anthony's mother, 'so don't get ideas of keeping it.'

'Oh! All right,' said Anthony. 'But we can keep it tonight can't we?'

'Yes,' said his mother. 'And tomorrow I'll ask around.'

Next day Anthony's mother asked her neighbours but no one had any knowledge of a Siamese kitten. Even the newspaper girl said she knew of no Siamese cats in the area.

'We can keep it then,' said Anthony. 'I'm going to call him Yowler.'

His mother was a little uncertain. She had a vague memory of reading somewhere that Siamese kittens were different from ordinary ones and more troublesome. For two days, all went well. Then, on the third day Anthony found the kitten had been accidentally shut in the best bedroom. He also noticed that on the carpet was an overturned plant pot, two broken ornaments and a significant wet patch. Anthony's mother took it very well, really, but she was less tolerant on the day when Yowler broke the special flower vase and she was quite angry when she found the slashed edges on the easy chairs where Yowler had tried out his claws.

'That kitten will have to go,' she said.

'Oh, give him a chance,' said Anthony. 'He has to learn how to behave.'

The next night, Anthony stayed up late watching television. His mother felt so tired after three hours of baking and cleaning that she went to bed soon after Anthony. They were expecting Anthony's father home on leave next day and they were both excited. Anthony seemed to have been asleep a short time (actually it was two hours) when he awoke to find Yowler making his strange yowling noise on his bed.

'Be quiet, Yowler,' said Anthony. 'You'll wake Mum.'

Yowler still made his yowling cries and appeared quite excited. Then Anthony noticed a smell of burning. He rushed downstairs and found the kitchen full of smoke. He switched off the electricity and then shouted to his mother. The oven was smoking furiously. It took a long time to clear the smoke and even longer to clean the oven next day before Dad arrived.

'You know,' said Anthony's mother, 'if Yowler hadn't warned us about the smoke in the kitchen, we might have had a real fire. He's earned his place in this family.'

So Yowler stayed; and Dad was pleased when he came home. He liked cats, too.

Prayer/Thought

Pets can bring happiness to many people, especially families with young children and people who may be lonely. If we do have a pet we should always remember that it is our responsibility to care for it properly. We should never have pets if we are not prepared to give them time and affection.

Assembly ideas

Children talk about their own pets—dog, cat, rabbit, etc. and say how they care for them.

Group dramatizations to demonstrate the responsibility of caring for a pet. For example, the pet shop purchase and later the abandoned cat, or teasing a dog so that it becomes bad-tempered. Compare with the correct way of treating a pet animal and how to train it to fit in the family.

Activity and discussion ideas

If you found an abandoned kitten on your doorstep and you knew that your mother hated cats, what would you do?

Which animals are the best pets for school and for home?

Some people say that many kittens on sale in pet shops often end up unwanted by the families that bought them. What do you think of this and is there anything that can be done to stop unwanted pets being thrown out?

14.3 Lampo the Railway Dog

Railway timetables are not the easiest things to follow—especially if the traveller is changing trains. Many people find that most difficult; yet there was once a dog who appeared quite confident when travelling by train—all by itself. It happened in Italy some years ago.

The ordinary-looking white mongrel dog was first seen when he jumped from a goods train onto the platform at Campiglia in north-west Italy. He trotted over to the water fountain, had a good long drink, then he walked to the office of the Assistant Station Master and dropped down in one corner seeming to say,

'Well, here I am. Home.'

The Assistant Station Master, Elvio Barlettani, let the dog stay in the office until his shift finished, then as he prepared for home, the white dog got up and followed him to his house. There, Elvio's little girl said: 'What a lovely present.'

So that was that. The dog stayed. They decided to call the dog Lampo. Next morning, Lampo accompanied the little girl to school; and he did that every morning. But what was most interesting was what Lampo did after leaving the school. He always went to the railway station and waited for a train. He travelled mostly on passenger trains and he was particularly fond of express trains. Every night, Lampo came back to Elvio's house; no matter how far he travelled. Elvio wondered where Lampo went in the trains so he asked his friends at the other stations and on the trains to watch out for the white dog. They reported that Lampo often travelled hundreds of kilometres and even changed trains. The remarkable thing was that the dog seemed to know which trains he needed; and he always came back to Campiglia.

Unfortunately, the Station Master found out about Lampo and he wasn't very pleased.

'No stray dog is allowed on the Italian railways,' he said, 'and dogs are certainly not allowed in the railway office. Get it out—and quick.'

So Lampo had to go. The problem was, where? You see, he had to go so far away that he wouldn't find his way back to Campiglia. Sadly, Elvio arranged for a friend hundreds of kilometres away to give Lampo a new home and the dog was handed over to the railway guard to deliver to the distant station.

Elvio's little daughter was heartbroken—so much so that her father promised to get her a puppy for her birthday; but the little girl only wanted Lampo.

It was several days later that a report came into the railway office that a white dog had been seen jumping on trains in the area where Lampo had his new home. More reports came in of the white dog riding on trains; and Elvio was sure it must be Lampo because the places where the dog was sighted were on the route to Campiglia. It took a long time; but eventually Lampo did get back. The story made headlines in the newspapers and Lampo became famous. He appeared on television and Elvio wrote a book about him called *Lampo the Travelling Dog*. They even put up a monument to Lampo on his home station in Campiglia.

Prayer/Thought
Animals without proper homes should always be treated with kindness. They may not appear to be attractive because no one cares for them; but they may be remarkable animals like Lampo the railway dog.

Assembly ideas
The legend of Gelert (Beddgelert).
Working dogs: sheepdog, husky, guide dog, police dog.

Activity and discussion ideas
On a local train timetable, travel down five stations, then work out the time of the first train back to the start.
How would you housetrain a fully grown dog or cat who had never lived in a house before?

15 HARVEST

15.1 The Invisible Harvest Festival Gift

Colin always liked harvest time in the country; and he looked forward each year to the Harvest Festival in the village church. Every year he tried to bring something he had grown or worked for himself. One year it was a giant marrow—that was when he had entered his marrow for the village show and got the second prize. Another year it was six new-laid brown eggs. Now this year it was not so easy. The family had moved to another house and the garden had been neglected so nothing was ready for harvest. Colin's father had been out of work for a time so there was no money to buy anything. So, one day, when Colin went to visit his grandpa he didn't look his usual cheerful self; and Grandpa noticed it.

'What's the matter, Colin?' he asked.

'Oh, nothing,' said Colin.

'I can see something's worrying you,' said Grandpa.

'Oh, it's the harvest,' said Colin. 'I can't think of anything to take to church.'

'Ah,' said Grandpa, 'that's where you'll have to use your brains. That's God's gift to you. You use 'em to find out how to thank God for all you have.'

Colin left his Grandpa's cottage and walked along the lane towards his home. He decided to take a short cut through the woods. It was one of his favourite walks. He could watch the pheasants walking near the keeper's rearing cages, looking for food. Now one of those birds would look good in the Harvest Service. But he couldn't take one of them. There were strict laws about poaching pheasants; and besides, his uncle was the gamekeeper. It was an old wood and there were fallen trees everywhere. Suddenly the idea came to him. He could drag out some of the smaller branches and chop them up for Grandpa's winter log pile.

That evening, Colin returned to Grandpa's cottage. The old

man was out so Colin took a quick look in the shed. The pile of logs was very low indeed; so he would appreciate a few sacks for harvest time. Colin began to walk home; and on the way he met his Grandpa carrying a few sticks for his fire.

'Hello,' said Colin. 'I see you got a bit of wood there.'

'I have to keep a bit of fire,' said Grandpa.

When Colin got home, he told his father about his idea for harvest time. His father thought it was a good one and said that he often wondered how the old man got through the winter when he couldn't afford coal. Next day, Colin started for the woods as soon as he had finished tea. First of all he cut some wood for his own home. His mother always liked larch to get the fire burning quickly. Then he looked around for some thicker branches to cut for logs. He soon had a great heap; and then came the really hard work. The branches were too thick for the axe so he used his father's wood saw. He worked until it was so dark he couldn't see to saw properly. Wearily he walked home and crawled into bed. Next day, after school, he continued with the work. After a week, he could see that his pile of logs was so big that he would have to start moving some in order to make room for some more sawing. He had a sack, so he began to drag the loaded sack through the woods and along the track to his Grandpa's shed.

'What's this?' said Grandpa when he saw the logs.

'It's my harvest gift,' said Colin.

'Well, well,' said Grandpa.

For another two weeks Colin carried on working and carrying the logs to Grandpa's shed. Then it was Harvest Festival in the church. Colin went with all the boys from school. He was the only one not carrying something to the service. They all stared at him.

'Where's your harvest gift, Colin?' said one boy.

Colin didn't reply and walked on into the church. It was filled with the fruits of harvest. Sheaves of corn were tied to the pillars. There were loaves of bread and great heaps of vegetables. The other children carried their gifts to the front. Colin looked at his blistered hands and thought of the backbreaking work he had done. He was happy about his harvest gift; and someone else was happy, too. Grandpa.

Prayer/Thought
We are thankful for the harvest of corn and berries, and all the good things our farmers and gardeners grow. May we remember, as we eat our food, that many people have worked hard to produce it.

Assembly ideas
Harvest Festival service.
Harvest presentation with groups—choral speech, harvest rhymes, miming harvest activities.

Activity and discussion ideas
Make bread and corn dollies.
Write a harvest prayer or a harvest song.
How does the harvesting in Britain today differ from a hundred years ago?
Find out about the work of Oxfam in helping to feed more people in other countries.
What are 'natural foods'?
How do you think school dinners could be improved?

15.2 The Mystery of the Harvest Rearranger

The normally quiet little village in the Sussex Downs was strangely alive and buzzing with excitement. A bird's-eye view would immediately show that all the activity centred on the village church. The church was hundreds of years old with the tower almost completely covered with ivy. But just at that moment, it was the inside of the church which was being covered—with all the things for the Harvest Thanksgiving next day. Men, women and children were bringing their harvest produce—big fat marrows, huge potatoes, beetroot, eggs, cakes, turnips, cabbages bigger than the biggest cooking pot you ever saw, onions as big as cricket balls and every kind of vegetable you could think of. There were flowers—masses of them. The workers in the church were trying to make the display better than any other year. The vicar's wife was planning and putting the last touches to the display. When it was all in place, everyone heaved a sigh of relief and they all agreed that it did look better than ever before. So everyone went home and the church was locked up and left in darkness and silence.

Next morning, the vicar's wife went with her little girl and boy to look at the church decorations and make any last minute rearrangement. As soon as they were through the door, the vicar's wife could sense that something had happened: something was different.

'Look, Mummy,' said the little girl. 'Someone has been changing things. The roses are moved back and the sunflowers are in front. And the new bread is behind the blackberries. Who could have done it? It is still pretty, isn't it?'

'I don't think so,' said her mother. 'Whoever put those ugly potatoes right in the middle of that display; and just that one egg there where we had those beautiful rosy apples from Mr Whitaker.'

Then, quite quickly, the anger faded from her face and she said in a very quiet voice, 'Yes, it is still beautiful; perhaps even more so.'

For the vicar's wife had suddenly realized who had given the potatoes and the blackberries and the one speckled brown egg. Then she said: 'I wonder who could have altered it? It must be someone who knows the people well.'

It was someone who knew the people well indeed. During the night, someone stole into the church, opening the door with a key and, with the aid of a torch, changed things around a bit. That new bread was given by the local baker—but he gave it as a sort of advertisement so that everyone would come to him to buy more bread; but the blackberries were gathered by two children who missed going on a picnic in order to pick them fresh for the Thanksgiving. The roses were moved back behind the sunflowers. Those roses came from the big house where the squire liked to think that he was the only man who knew how to grow roses. But it was his gardener who actually looked after the rose beds; and the squire was so mean that he never gave anything away unless it was for a display where he hoped that people would say 'What fine roses. Grown by the squire of course.' But the sunflowers came from the garden of a man crippled by arthritis so that he couldn't work like he used to; so his garden was wild. He loved sunflowers so that was the only flower he grew. He gave some to the Thanksgiving so that other people could share them. The potatoes came from an old widow who dug up all the last ones in her little garden and gave them all to the church.

So, for the next hour, the man (for it was a man) went about the church rearranging the things according to their importance, and not their appearance. He seemed to know where everything came from; and he seemed to know every nook and cranny in the building. No one ever saw who it was that altered the decorations in the church for that Thanksgiving Day. The vicar's wife knew; but she never told anyone.

Prayer/Thought
There is a story in the Bible about the widow's mite where a woman gave one small coin but it was worth quite a lot to her because she was so poor. When people give to a good cause in a street collection, no matter how much or how little is given, they all receive the same kind of receipt—probably a little sticker badge.

Assembly ideas
The food chain.
Natural foods and food from the hedgerow, food from the sea; processing food, cleanliness of food.
School dinners.
The corn dolly.

Activity and discussion ideas
What cereal do you eat for breakfast? How does each packet of cereal get to the shops?
What foods, eaten at tea-time, come from other countries and how do they get to our shops?

15.3 The Magic of Music

In South America there is a brown-skinned, black-haired people called the Guarani. They tell a story about their wonderful harvest many years ago when Father Francis, a Roman Catholic priest, came to the village to try and help the people to a better life. He found the villagers were a happy lot but they suffered from near starvation when the rains came. They lived in leaky huts and suffered from many tropical illnesses. Father Francis showed them how to build strong houses which were watertight. Then they all helped to build a church. At first they all worked hard at building; but after a while most of the men were bored and went off hunting. Still, they managed to finish off enough houses and the church was complete. One thing they all loved; and that was to play the musical instruments Father Francis had brought from Spain. They had a violin, a lute and a cornet. Whenever the music was played in the church they all trooped in and joined in the service.

One day, Father Francis gathered a few men to go with him to collect some of the cobs of wild maize. They collected all day until their baskets were full and heavy. Then they brought all the maize cobs into the courtyard where the cobs were spread to dry before being loaded into the priest's storehouse.

'Why, there's more than enough corn there to feed you for a whole year, Señor,' said one of the men. 'We could have fetched more later. Why did you get us to gather so much all at once?'

'If we use it properly,' said Father Francis, 'it will feed not only me, but the whole village.'

'Whatever do you mean?' asked the villager.

'After the rains, I will show you what is to be done,' said the priest.

For the next few weeks, most of the men went hunting; but a few stayed in the village where the priest showed them how to make rough spades in the crude forge that he had constructed. When everything was ready, several days later, Father Francis called all the people to a meeting in the church. He told them that he would show them how the seed they had gathered could be increased a hundredfold so that all could have food. He then called for volunteers to come out and work. As soon as he said the word 'work', half the villagers disappeared. Eventually only ten men said they would help. So Father Francis led his little band to a patch of land where a bush fire had cleared trees and vegetation. There the priest showed his ten men how to dig the rich brown soil. For three days the men toiled in the hot sun; and the strip of cultivated brown earth slowly grew larger; but Father Francis was not satisfied. Next morning, just before sunrise, the village awoke to the sound of music. They all got out of bed and ran to the church where the music of the violin, lute and cornet soon had them singing hymns. Then, at the end of the service, Father Francis led the musicians outside and along a trail. All the people followed—all the men and the children. They came to the little strip of cultivated land where, gleaming in the sun, all the home-made spades were laid on the ground. The musicians played on as the first of the volunteers picked up his spade and ran to carry on with his digging. The next volunteer followed, then the next and the next until the tenth man took his spade. The musicians played louder than ever. Another man took a spade, then another and another. Soon all the men had a spade as the whole village began to work on the patch. The men did the hard digging; and the women who had now joined them with the children cleared the stones and tree stumps. It was hard work but no one grumbled because, all the time, the musicians played; and they played all the way back to the village that night. Next day the musicians led the villagers out to the patch again. This time the people worked happily even when the music stopped. The musicians played during their lunch break and the walk home. So, day after day, Father Francis got his willing workers cultivating the patch. He showed them how to sow the seed. They saw the seedlings grow and they hoed the weeds. Then, finally, came the harvest—with music all the time they were working. So much corn came in that their storehouses were not big enough. More buildings and more hard work; but this time they didn't grumble.

Prayer/Thought

There are many people in Britain and in other countries whose lives could be so much easier and happier with our help; but some people do not easily accept help when it is offered. There is usually a way to gain their confidence if we try long enough.

Assembly ideas
Harvest—how others live; how others die.
The farmer.
The work of Oxfam.
Christian Aid pamphlets 'Food for all' and 'Happiness of fair shares'.

Activity and discussion ideas
Make up a list of 'Thank you' things.
Are there any lonely old folk living near the school who would appreciate a harvest parcel of useful things? What might the parcel contain?

16 CHRISTMAS

16.1 It Really Came True

John and his sister Katie were coming home from school one dark afternoon in December and they were talking about what their teacher had been saying at the end of the day's lessons. The children were twins and they were in the same class.

'I think we could find somebody we could help near our house,' said Katie.

'Who?' said John.

'I don't know. Somebody.'

At that moment they both looked at the house they were passing. It had no lights on but they could see the flickering flames from the fire which showed through the window of a dark room; and they both thought of the same thing (as twins do sometimes).

'We'll go and see Mrs Cyno,' they both said together.

They ran up the little path to the front door and John knocked.

There was no answer. John knocked again, this time quite loudly. They could hear the squeak and bump of a chair being moved back and then the footsteps of an old person slowly walking to the door. The door opened and there was Mrs Cyno—old, frail and bowed. She didn't know the twins so they introduced themselves and asked Mrs Cyno if she wanted anything done.

'Why yes, my dears,' she said. 'I want some things from the shop. I haven't been able to get out for two days because me leg is so bad. You could fetch me these few things.'

While Katie went off to the shop, John found himself a job in the shed chopping up some wood for the fire. Then he filled both buckets with coal.

'Is there anything else you want doing, Mrs Cyno?' he asked.

'That will do nicely for now,' said the old lady, 'so perhaps you can wait here for your sister by the fire. She shouldn't be long.'

Very soon, Katie was back and the two children carried on home. Their mother was a bit angry at first when they arrived home so late; but when she knew where they had been she was quite pleased and she told them all she knew about Mrs Cyno.

'She lost her son many years ago. He just walked out of the house and was never heard of again. The old lady has no other relatives as far as we know. People do call and see her but she gets very lonely. She will be feeling sad now because it is getting near Christmas and she has so little to look forward to.'

'Perhaps we can do something to make her happy,' said John.

The children did call once or twice after that; but it was now so near Christmas that they forgot about Mrs Cyno until one night much later. It was Christmas Eve and their mother said that she would have to go to their aunt for a short time and sort out the Christmas presents for their young cousins. Father was out too. He had gone to see Grandma in the next town. So Katie and John were left alone in the house. Only minutes after mother had left, there was a knock on the door. The children had been told to be very careful about opening the door at night when they were alone. The knocking was repeated.

'I'll just go and see who it is,' said John.

'All right,' said Katie, who was stirring the soup they were just about to eat for supper.

When John opened the door he saw the dirtiest, scruffiest man he had ever imagined.

'Can you give me something to eat?' said the stranger.

John looked at the man. His face looked kindly, even though it was dirty.

'You can share our soup,' he said on impulse.

So the man came in and they shared out the soup and they had some of the new rolls that their mother had baked that day. The man was obviously hungry because he finished his soup in half the time that John took; so Katie found some cheese and the stranger ate that too. It was just at that moment that John had an idea; so he signalled to Katie to the other side of the room and whispered his plan to her.

'You remember Mrs Cyno and her lost son?' he whispered.

'Why, yes,' said Katie.

'Well,' said John, 'why don't we get this man to pretend to be her son and he could stay with her and make her happy this Christmas?'

'What a good idea,' said Katie. 'I'm sure he'll agree because he said he had nowhere to sleep tonight and he doesn't mind where he goes.'

So the children explained about the old lady and their plan to pretend that he was her lost son. When they asked him if he would do it, he didn't say anything. So Katie asked him again because she thought perhaps he hadn't heard properly. This time he just nodded. John and Katie went with him to Mrs Cyno's house and knocked on the door. They could just see her inside; and as usual she had no light on but the fire was burning brightly. John knocked again, this time quite loudly. Mrs Cyno slowly got up and dragged her weary way to the door and opened it just a little.

'Oh,' she said, 'it's you, John and Katie. I am pleased to see you.'

'We have brought someone to see you,' said Katie, and then she stopped.

The stranger walked in and opened his arms; and Mrs Cyno opened her arms too. Then they were hugging each other and John thought he could hear Mrs Cyno crying.

'It doesn't look like a pretend meeting,' said John to Katie. 'It looks real to me.'

And it was. The man *was* Mrs Cyno's son—home just in time for Christmas. Mrs Cyno said it was her Christmas miracle.

Prayer/Thought

At this time of year we should spare a thought for members of our own family who may feel lonely and cut off. It could be that our cheerfulness could help them and even one visit could make them happier.

Assembly ideas

Groups singing special carols; acting short plays about Christmas and giving; Christmas customs.

Activity and discussion ideas

Christmas mural.

Design a Christmas card with a special message for old people.

Write your own Christmas words as extra verses to a tune you know.

Discuss 'Do we ever give people another chance when they let us down?'

Get answers from different people to the question 'What are the most important things in life?'

16.2 Terry and the Christmas Tree

It was just a few weeks to Christmas when Terry said he thought Christmas trees all came from Woolworths. Terry was just four years old and he was a spastic, unable to move without his wheelchair. He lived in a town and he had never seen a pine tree growing. His older brother, Chris, told him that Christmas trees grew in a wood.

Mick said, 'They grow in thousands. I'll take you to see them one day.'

Mick was a friend of Terry's brother. He had a car, an old banger, on which he spent his spare time when he finished work at the garage. Terry was fond of Mick who always gave him bolts and nuts to manipulate and so strengthen his weak hands.

Terry never forgot about the Christmas trees; and every day he talked about going to see them. The next Saturday Mick finished early at the garage, so Chris put Terry in the car and they both stared out of the windows as Mick drove out of town and into a country lane. There Mick stopped the car because he said that his boss had told him that the landowner, Mr Bosworth, didn't like cars parked on his land because he was always watching for thieves taking his trees.

Mick and Chris pushed Terry's wheelchair along the lane and through a gateway into a muddy field. It was rough work pushing Terry in his chair. He was nearly jolted out. Everything creaked and groaned; and Terry's teeth began to rattle. But he was so excited he never noticed the rough journey.

Suddenly they stopped and Terry shouted, 'Eh. I can see 'em.'

There must have been a thousand little trees, none more than two metres tall.

Terry said, 'They aren't silver.'

'Well, fancy saying that,' said Mick, 'just when we brought you all this way.'

'I want one,' said Terry.

'You're too early boy-o,' said Mick. 'Christmas is weeks away.'

'Can I have one for Christmas then?' Terry asked.

'Oh yes,' they both promised.

'Which one?' asked Terry.

So Mick had to walk along the first row until Terry pointed out the tree he fancied. It was a beauty, well-shaped and just that much bigger than the others.

'O.K.,' said Mick, 'we'll push off now.'

And he grabbed the wheelchair and got Terry away before he could change his mind about waiting for that tree.

Well, after that, not a day passed without Terry talking about his tree. All the neighbours heard about it. The man next door bought a pot to put the tree in. Sandra, Terry's sister, bought him pretty baubles nearly every day when she came home from work. Terry kept them in a box near his bed. He was so proud of them.

Next Saturday Terry said he wanted to see his tree again; and he wanted to hang a bauble, a silver ball, right on the top to show it was his tree. Of course Mick said he would take him. It was muddier than ever on the field; but Terry was even more excited than before; and when Mick fixed the silver ball right at the top of the tree Terry nearly cried with joy.

'It looks smashing,' he whispered.

'Just one more week, boy-o,' said Mick, 'and we'll come with a spade to dig it up for you.'

The next Saturday, Chris pushed Terry to the garage and went to find Mick. There was no one in the garage. It was miserably cold so Chris lifted Terry into Mick's car thinking they could wait there until Mick came back. It was then that he saw the note in Mick's handwriting 'Gone to a breakdown. Back at 4.00 p.m.' Chris hadn't the heart to tell Terry that they would have to go back home without the tree. He had an idea.

'Listen, Terry. Mick has gone off on a job. He says I can drive his car. O.K.?'

'Yes. Let's go,' said Terry.

So Chris, just seventeen and without a driving licence, drove Mick's car carefully through the back streets, avoiding any places where a policeman could spot him. He was quite a capable driver because he had driven the car before on the spare ground next to the garage; but he still had a strange feeling in his tummy as he drove. They soon came to the lane where the car could be parked. Then the hard journey with Terry's chair up the slope of the field. Chris was breathing hard when they reached the top; and Terry was leaning forward in his excitement so that the chair nearly toppled over. They looked and saw—nothing. There *was* something, but not trees—just the stumps sticking up out of the ground.

'He's cut 'em all down,' shouted Chris.

Terry never said anything. He just stared; and a large tear trickled down his cheek. They were both so absorbed that neither saw the two men approaching. One was a policeman who said:

'Is that your car parked in the lane?'

'Yes,' said Chris.

'You don't look old enough to have a licence,' said the policeman. 'Have you got one?'

'No,' said Chris.

So that was that. Anyway, it soon became clear that the policeman and the owner of the wood were trying to trace the people who had stolen the trees. They had all been cut down during the night and loaded on a lorry.

By this time poor Terry was really crying.

The policeman said, 'What's he crying for?'

So Chris explained about Terry's tree; and he could see that the policeman and the landowner were looking really sorry for Terry.

'I've got an idea,' said the policeman. 'You said that the tree was growing bigger and bigger. Well, I think I know where your tree is.'

'Where?' asked Terry.

'Why, the mayor has it,' said the policeman, 'right outside the Town Hall. You can tell it by your silver ball at the top. You come and see it.'

So they all crushed into Mick's car and the policeman drove it back to town. When they came to the square near the Town Hall Terry shouted out:

'That's it. Look, there's my silver ball right at the top.'

Well, it was the same kind of ball, so they all agreed that it must be his tree. After that, the policeman took them home and warned Chris's parents that he might have to take action about driving without a licence but he would try to keep it out of the case book. He gave a stern warning about driving without a licence, then he left. Chris's father was angry about the driving; and he had something else to be mad about when he discovered that his spade had been left in the field. Mick was mad, too, about having his car taken away and thinking it was stolen. Poor Chris really caught it; but Terry was as pleased as a dog with six tails. Every day somebody pushed his chair to the square; and there he would sit, just looking at that tree. After a week, everyone was sick of it—except Terry.

When the tree was finally taken down, Terry asked the council workmen to give him his silver ball. And they did.

Prayer/Thought

Preparations for Christmas are often a good test of everyone's patience because so much extra work has to be done before the holiday. The load for parents can be lightened when children help.

Assembly ideas

The mince pie—origin. Ingredients and countries of origin.

How Joseph Mohr and Francis Gruber came to write 'Silent Night'.

Activity and discussion ideas

What things should go on the Christmas tree?

Pretend to be the innkeeper and give your account of the Nativity story.

What Christmas decorations could be made for school which could be given away to someone whose life is dull and miserable?

16.3 Hughie's Tree

The little Scottish village was very, very trim, with a place for everything and everything in its place. Everyone in the village worked all day without a smile. They all worked hard but never seemed to have any fun. No one was ever heard to sing: except in the music lesson at school. It was a dull place. December came and several days later there was no sign of Christmas anywhere in the village.

It was the middle of the month when Hughie came out of hospital. On his first day home he had a visitor; it was his friend Anna who lived next door.

'I'll have to lie here in bed, day after day, for a whole month just looking at that fir tree outside the window,' he said.

'Look,' said Anna, who was trying to cheer him up. 'I've had an idea to keep you busy.'

She showed Hughie what she had brought. There were lots of pine cones, bits of silver and gold foil and a doll with blonde hair.

'Mother says dolls are a waste of money,' said Anna.

Anna's father was the village grocer who thought that a lot more things were a waste of money.

Hughie and Anna made decorations night after night whilst Anna's mother wondered what mischief they were up to. Anna's mother didn't approve of her daughter going so often to see Hughie. She thought it was wasting time and that Anna should be studying.

'But Hughie so looks forward to Anna's visits,' said Hughie's mother.

Sometimes Anna's little brother Richard and young sister Susan went with her to Hughie's because they were helping to collect bottle tops, silver and gold wrapping paper and old electric light bulbs. They also helped to fetch coloured foil from the milk-bottling factory. But Richard and Susan were never allowed to see what Anna and Hughie were making.

'It is a secret,' said Anna.

The bottle tops were threaded on long strings, the old light bulbs were painted in bright reds, blues, greens and yellows. Anna cut out wings and clothes to make the old doll into a shining angel.

'What if it rains and spoils the clothes?' said Anna.

'Of course it won't rain,' said Hughie. 'It will never rain on Christmas Eve.'

At last it *was* Christmas Eve. The village street was deserted and all the shops were shut. There was no late opening in the village because the shopkeepers said it was a waste. Everyone was at home wrapping up presents in ordinary brown wrapping paper because it would come in useful to be used again. Anna sneaked out of the house carrying a big stepladder; and no one saw her.

It was Susan who first saw the magic sight.

'Look at Hughie's tree,' she shouted as she ran outside towards the tree festooned with all the decorations Hughie and Anna had made in those evenings together.

Little Richard rushed out to see the tree, followed by his mother who could only say: 'What a waste! What a waste!' over and over again.

Soon all the children and their parents were outside Hughie's house looking at the decorated fir tree. All the grown-ups said: 'What a waste! What a waste!'

Hughie looked out of his window and looked at the tree. It wasn't a waste to him.

The children shouted, 'What a lovely waste!'

Anna's father didn't say it was a waste at all. He just stared at the fir tree for a long time; then he said:

'It's really good; but it needs just a bit extra. It needs some snow.'

'Snow,' said the children. 'What snow?'

Then they started to sing the carol they had once learned at school, years ago.

'You'll see,' said the grocer, as he went off to see his friend the chemist.

The carol singing now spread to the grown-ups. Nobody thought to say it was a waste again. They had sung three carols, or as much of them as they could remember (for they hadn't sung a carol for years), when Anna's father came back with a load of cotton wool. He had bought every bit in the chemist's shop and he covered the tall fir tree with cotton wool snow from top to bottom. He worked on and on until it was quite late and Anna's mother came to see if anything nasty had happened to him.

'There,' he said, when it was finished, 'that's a proper Christmas tree. We'll have one here every year.'

And they did.

Prayer/Thought

A dull Christmas time can be transformed by the enthusiasm of children—especially when they remember that it is not just a time for receiving presents, but a time for giving; and the best gift to give others is kindness.

Assembly ideas

Christmas legends from other countries. Information from *The World of Christmas* by Loundes and Kailer.

Activity and discussion ideas

'Christmas is coming'—What does that mean to you?

If you were ill in bed at Christmastime, what would you want to cheer you up, a tree or something different?

Would you rather have longer holidays at Christmas or in summer? Why?

Think of ways to make other people happy at Christmas.

16.4 Christmas Was a Baby

On December 23rd, 1964, a baby girl was born just a few kilometres north of Jerusalem. She was a beautiful baby with fair hair and blue eyes. Her parents and her seven older brothers and sisters all agreed that only one name was possible for her—'Christmas', which in the local language was 'Miladdie'.

When Miladdie was just one week old she had a very bad cold which affected her eyes. Her mother took the baby to the clinic where the nurse made up a prescription of drops to treat Miladdie's eyes. Unfortunately Miladdie's mother had a similar bottle at home which contained iodine; and she accidentally put the wrong drops in the baby's eyes. Miladdie screamed with pain; and at first her mother couldn't think what was wrong. When she realized what had happened she snatched up the baby and ran to the hospital. It was too late. Miladdie was blind in both eyes. The doctor advised the mother to take Miladdie to the Home for Blind Girls in the hope that, when she was older, an operation could restore some of her sight. At first the mother would not agree; but six months later she did take Miladdie to the Home for Blind Girls in Jerusalem. So the little baby girl became the youngest child ever to go to the Blind Home. Friends of the Home provided a cot, pram, playpen, high chair, rocking horse and toys to make Miladdie happy. She started talking and walking; and she was loved by all the children.

Nearly all the blind children went back to their own families for holidays; but Miladdie's parents never came for little 'Christmas'.

The Blind Home was visited by tourists quite often when they came to Jerusalem. One party of tourists was rather special, for they were mostly blind people. One couple said that although they had been married a long time, they had no children and they wished to adopt a child from the Home. The man was totally blind but his wife had good sight so they said they could bring up a child of any age. They chose Miladdie.

As the Principal of the Home kissed Miladdie goodbye, she wondered whether she had done the right thing. Miladdie's parents had agreed immediately for her to go to the English couple; but Miladdie was six years old and she didn't speak the same language as her new foster parents and she was going to a strange country with a different climate and customs. Would it work out all right?

A few days later a letter came from Miladdie's new mother which said that little Christmas was happily settled and she had found some friends to play with. Then a few weeks later there was a telephone call to the Principal of the Blind Girls' Home. Miladdie had been playing with her new daddy and suddenly she had struck him in the face just above his eyes. Suddenly he could see—for the first time in twenty years. He could see his pretty young daughter, Miladdie the Christmas baby; and she had given him the best present he could ever wish for—sight.

Prayer/Thought

At Christmastime we should spare a thought for the children in other countries who may be handicapped. Many families in North Africa are too poor to support a blind person; but in a special Home, the blind child can learn a trade so that he is able to earn a living later on.

Assembly ideas

Christian Aid Assembly Suggestions—'It's not fair'.

Activity and discussion ideas

What sort of things could the school do to raise money for a Christmas charity?

What local organizations do something special for the aged or crippled at Christmas? What do they do?

Other teacher's books of interest from Ward Lock Educational

A Book for Assemblies in Secondary and Middle Schools Guy Williams 0 7062 3816 8

This practical handbook is intended as a valuable resource for the teacher facing the problem of finding material for assemblies. It offers an anthology of well-loved readings for pupils of all faiths and backgrounds. Assemblies relevant to particular seasons are included, such as the pre-Christmas and Easter periods, as well as material suitable for use throughout the year.

The Living Religions Series

Each book clearly states the basic beliefs of the religion discussed and explores its historical and cultural aspects.

Roman Catholocism
Buddhism
Hinduism
Humanism
Islam
Judaism
Living Tribal Religions

The Orthodox Church
Protestant Christian Churches
Jehovah's Witnesses
Mormons and Christian Scientists
The Baha'i Faith
Sikhism

Practical Classroom Organization in the Primary School Michael Bassey 0 7062 3665 3

Advice and information given here will remedy some of the difficulties encountered by student and inexperienced teachers in their school work. Soundly based in theory, the book is full of practical advice on such questions as methods of maintaining discipline and of organizing work.

Festive Occasions in the Primary School

Redvers Brandling   0 7062 3746 3

This practical resource book provides helpful information about 'occasions' such as St. Valentine's Day, Easter, Midsummer, Harvest, Hallowe'en and Christmas, which all feature prominently in the primary school calendar. They are dealt with in a wealth of detail which includes related facts and fancies; a selection of relevant poems and stories; appropriate practical activities, ideas for display, drama and visits, and finally suggestions for class assembly presentations.

A Book of Practical Ideas for the Primary School *Redvers Brandling*   0 7062 3884 2

Here is a pot pourri of over 120 practical and educationally valuable activities for the primary school teacher to use in and outside the classroom. The contents of this book include work on codes, word puzzles, messages, mime and drama, outdoor games and activities, collecting and making things, and purposeful games involving mathematical work, talking, writing, listening and movement.

The Story Teller 2

Compiled by Graham Barrett and Michael Morpurgo

This book contains a selection of stories for teachers and parents to read aloud to children in the ten to fourteen age range. The stories have been specially chosen for this age group and they include contributions by such notable authors as Ursula Moray Williams, William Golding, Frank O'Connor, Katherine Mansfield, Charles Causley, Roald Dahl, W. Somerset Maugham and Raymond Williams. The range and variety of the selection will undoubtedly stimulate young listeners and hopefully encourage a deeper and wider appreciation of books and reading.

0 7062 3801 X